SCHLOSS II

More Fascinating Royal History of German Castles

SUSAN SYMONS

Published by Roseland Books
The Old Rectory, St Just-in-Roseland, Truro, Cornwall, TR2 5JD

Copyright ©2015 Susan Symons

ISBN 13: 978-0-9928014-1-0
ISBN 10: 0-9928014-1-9

For my mother, Joan Greenwood, with many thanks for a lifetime of support and encouragement.

CONTENTS

1

INTRODUCTION

In July 2013 the small town of Saalfeld, in the heart of Germany, celebrated the birth of Prince George of Cambridge (the great-grandson of Queen Elizabeth II and third in line to the British throne). His birth was covered in the local newspapers, and the town's brewmaster brewed a special Prince George's Beer. Saalfeld is a long way from London (where Prince George was born), but to its twenty-eight thousand inhabitants the prince is more than just a far-away royal celebrity. This is because Saalfeld played an important part in Prince George's ancestry. He is a direct descendant (the ten-times great-grandson) of Duke Johann Ernst, the builder of the town's baroque castle and the founder of the royal line of Saxe-Coburg. All this was explained to me very proudly when I visited Schloss Saalfeld in the course of researching this book. It illustrates both the fascinating royal history of German castles and the close interconnection between the British and German royal families. (To find out more about Saalfeld, please see chapter 6.)

Schloss is the German word for castle or palace, and wherever you are in Germany you are never very far from one of these. For most of its history Germany was not a single country but a decentralised federation of independent states. Right up until the end of the monarchy

1

in 1918 there were dozens of different kingdoms, duchies, and princi-palities, each with its own reigning family. These have left a mark in the thousands of castles and palaces that dot the German countryside. For anyone who is interested in royal history, or old buildings, or going sightseeing, Germany is a delight to visit.

I started to write about schlösser (the plural of schloss) after my husband and I visited Germany. We drove around the countryside, looking at some out-of-the-way places, and everywhere we went we visited some of the local schlösser, or castles and palaces. We saw some wonderful buildings in stunningly beautiful locations and also came across some dramatic and compelling stories of the German royal fam-ilies who built and lived in them, which can rival anything in a mod-ern-day television soap opera. We discovered that German schlösser are a lot of fun to visit.

This is my second book about schlösser, written after we toured the northern half of Germany, visiting the states of Lower Saxony, Schleswig-Holstein, Mecklenburg-Pomerania, Brandenburg, and Thuringia. You can follow our route on the map in appendix A. The book is set out with a chapter for each state and, within that, a section for each schloss. Over the course of our trip we saw twenty-five in all, many of which are not well known to visitors to Germany. The book is a write-up of our visits and what grabbed our attention about the history, architecture, or geography of each schloss. It also tells some colourful personal stories about the historical royal characters connected with them. As well as the main narrative on each schloss, I have included some supplementary information in italics where I think this could be of interest to the reader.

A precise translation of the word schloss into English would be castle. However, I have used the word more widely in this book to denote any castle, palace, or stately home that once belonged to any of Germany's historical royal families. From our visits, we came to appreciate the durability and adaptability of these buildings as they survived the cen-turies and changed to meet the current times. The schlösser included in this book range from fortified castles of the Middle Ages, such as Burg Stargard; to grand ceremonial palaces built in the eighteenth century in imitation of Louis XIV's Versailles, such as Neustrelitz; to stately homes from the nineteenth century, such as Reinhardsbrunn. The newest schloss in the book is Braunschweig, which was destroyed in World War II but rebuilt and reopened in 2007 and houses a shopping mall as well as a museum.

Because there were so many royal families, the pages of German history just abound with colourful royal characters with fascinating personal histories. Their stories are full of passion and illicit love, rivalry and thwarted ambition, tragedy and loss. Royalty have always been the celebrities of their day, and these stories from history can match any adventures of today's 'celebs' as reported in *Hello* magazine. The royal stories in this book include the princess from a tiny German state who used her body and her brains to become the ruler of the vast Russian empire; the prince who tried to run away from his brutal and bullying father and was forced as his punishment to witness the execution of the friend who had helped him; and the German Queen of England whose private life was so scandalous that she was refused admittance to her own coronation.

In these personal histories, we came across some recurring themes. I was amazed by the network of family connections that bound Europe's royal families together and how, often through dynastic claims established by marriage in previous generations, German princes took over the thrones of many other countries, including Great Britain.

Germany was the royal marriage market for all of Europe's monarchies and a sadder story was about the risks for princesses, who usually had no say in their choice of husband. Love had little place in the royal marriage market. The only career open for most German princesses was a dynastic arranged marriage to a foreigner, often while still a teenager. A few were fortunate in the outcome and had a genuinely happy marriage. But many, despite their wealth and position, must have been deeply unhappy, and some did not survive the ordeal of childbirth.

The History of Germany

The history of Germany is not familiar to most English readers and as a result can sometimes seem confusing. It is important to remember that until relatively recently Germany was not a single country but a federation of numerous states, each with its own ruler and royal family. This was the case right up until the end of World War I, when the monarchy came to an end and Germany became a republic.

For over eight hundred years until it was disbanded in 1806, the independent German states were held together as part of the Holy Roman Empire under an elected emperor. In the time of the Holy Roman Empire, there were hundreds of pieces of independent territory in what is modern-day Germany. During the Napoleonic Wars the numbers dramatically reduced until, by the time of the Congress of Vienna at the end of the wars in 1815, there were fewer then fifty.

A legacy of the struggle against Napoleon was a growing nationalist movement and in 1871 Germany was unified for the first time, when the remaining states joined together in the German Empire under a Prussian emperor. This lasted only until the end of World War I; in 1918 revolution swept across the German states, and all the royal rulers abdicated. The Weimar Republic was established the following year, but was under pressure from the start and lasted only until the seizure of power by the Nazis and the beginning of the Third Reich in 1933.

After Germany's defeat in World War II, the victorious Allies divided Germany into British, French, US, and Soviet zones of occupation. This division hardened in 1949 with the setting up of two separate countries, the Federal Republic of Germany (known as West Germany) and the German Democratic Republic (known as East Germany or the GDR). These were divided by an 'iron curtain' for forty years until the fall of communism and Germany was reunified into a single country in 1990.

Appendix D at the back of the book is a brief explanation of relevant aspects of German history.

Another recurring theme was the problem of inheritance and the division of family property among sons. We came across many stories of jealousy and sibling rivalry, including that of the younger son who took advantage of civil unrest to usurp his brother's throne. Often the only career open to landless younger sons was to become a soldier of fortune, fighting for money in a foreign army. Many German princes also lost their lives while still young.

I have a long-standing interest in European royal history, but our schloss tour made me focus on a new aspect that I had not thought much about before—the places where history happened. These schlösser were the venue for many important events in German history, and seeing them gave me a more vivid picture of the events and the characters than from just reading about them. I was completely gripped, for example, when reading the diary of the Duchess Augusta of Saxe-Coburg-Saalfeld (the grandmother of both Queen Victoria and Prince Albert) for 11 October 1806, in which she tells how she looked out of the window to see the body of Prince Luis Ferdinand of Prussia, slain in battle with Napoleon's troops, carried into the courtyard of Schloss Saalfeld.

This book is not intended as an academic study, and I have tried to make it easy to read and entertaining. I want to share my view that history need not be a dull subject and that royal history in particular is fascinating and fun. The contents of the book include a mixture of historical information and my own observations and impressions about each schloss included. These observations come from my experience of visiting each particular schloss on a particular day. I must stress that they are entirely personal; another visitor on a different day could have an entirely different experience. Also, this book is not a detailed travel guide and readers will need to consult the schlösser websites, their guide books or other information, for opening hours and directions.

The sources I have consulted for the historical information are shown in the notes section and the bibliography at the back of the book. I have tried to make the history as accurate as I can and would like to apologise for any inadvertent errors. Germany had numerous royal families, several of which are included in this book. To help the reader sort out who is who in each royal family and where they fit into the story, I have included some charts and family trees in appendix E. And there is a timeline in appendix C to help connect events and individuals across time and country borders.

This is my second book about the fascinating royal history of German schlösser. I wrote the first after taking a similar schloss tour a year earlier, in 2013.[1] From now on, to avoid confusion and distinguish between the two books, I shall call the present book *Schloss II* and my first book *Schloss I*. A list of all the schlösser included in both my books is in appendix B.

I would like to thank everyone who helped with this book, including Bearn Bilker, Ulf von Hielmcrone, Martin Modes, Joachim Ortlepp, Felix Sienknecht, and all the museum curators and attendants who welcomed us and patiently tried to answer my questions and to search out material for me in English. Thank you also to everyone in the tourist information offices, bakeries, and other places, who gave directions, suggested castles and palaces to visit, and were generally friendly to us. Not all of the schlösser had information available in English, and I also thank Cornelia Oldifredo for translating some of the German material I brought home.

I particularly want to thank my husband, Terry, who has helped in so many ways—by taking the photographs, chauffeuring me around Germany, brushing up on his rusty German, acting as a sounding board, and generally encouraging me to write both books. We have already enjoyed our third schloss tour, so please watch out for my third book on German schlösser.

I hope that you will enjoy my book and that it will encourage you to visit a schloss if ever you are in Germany. But beware—schloss hunting is rather like an infectious bug. Once you get it, as I have, it can be difficult to shake off.

Names and Titles of the German Royal Families

The hereditary titles of the rulers of the independent German states is another confusing area of German history, as these varied according to the size
and importance of the state. So a duke (herzog) was the ruler of a duchy; a
prince (fürst) of a principality, and a count (graf) of a county.

At the top of the rankings in the time of the Holy Roman Empire were
the prince electors (kurfürst). They were the rulers of the most important
German states, second in rank only to the Holy Roman emperor himself and
responsible for electing him.

No kingdoms were permitted within the Holy Roman Empire, as this
could threaten the prerogative of the emperor, so rulers who aspired to this
higher rank had to look outside its bounds. This can add to the confusion
with, for example, Elector Friedrich III of Brandenburg changing his title to
King Friedrich I in Prussia in 1701 and Elector Friedrich August I of Saxony
also becoming King August II of Poland in 1697.

When the Holy Roman Empire disbanded in 1806, there was a general
scramble among the ruling princes to upgrade their titles. So the principality
of Brunswick-Wolfenbüttel was elevated to the duchy of Brunswick around
this time, the duchy of Mecklenburg-Strelitz to a grand duchy, and the electorate of Hannover became a kingdom.

A further complication is that rulers often had the same first name, with
names such as Georg, Friedrich, and Wilhelm being popular. Every king of
Prussia, from 1701 when the title was created until the end of the monarchy
in 1918, was called either Friedrich, Wilhelm, or Friedrich Wilhelm.

2

LOWER SAXONY AND THE SCHAUMBURG-LIPPE AND OLDENBURG FAMILIES

Our schloss tour began in Lower Saxony in the northwest of Germany. This is one of the largest of the sixteen federal states, or länder, that make up Germany today. Lower Saxony borders the North Sea in the north and the Netherlands in the west; to the east and south it borders the other federal states that we would visit on our tour. After stops in Schleswig-Holstein, Mecklenburg-Western Pomerania, Brandenburg, and Thuringia, we would come back to end our trip in Lower Saxony, three weeks later.

In the nineteenth century, what today is Lower Saxony was made up of four independent states, each with its own reigning family. These were the kingdom of Hannover, the grand duchy of Oldenburg, the duchy of Brunswick, and the principality of Schaumburg-Lippe. In my first book, we visited schlösser associated with the kingdom of Hannover and discovered the fascinating story of how a German duke became king of England (see *Schloss I*, chapter 2). This time, we explored schlösser associated with the other three states and found some equally compelling royal stories. We started at Schloss Bückeburg in the south of Lower Saxony in what had been the principality of Schaumburg-Lippe. Here we found a talented family and a special place.

Bückeburg

Schloss Bückeburg is the ancestral home of the Schaumburg-Lippe family, who were the rulers of the principality of the same name. It turned out to be a wonderful choice for our first place to visit. Bückeburg has been in the ownership of the family throughout its history, and they still live in part of the schloss. It has survived the centuries intact, without suffering the same fate of destruction or severe neglect that we were to find with so many other schlösser. As a result of this continuity, Bückeburg is a special place—a treasure house of history and art. The whole history of the principality and its royal family is encompassed in this building, and we were fortunate enough to see it all as part of a perfect guided tour.

Schaumburg-Lippe may have been the smallest of the German principalities, covering just 131 square miles and having a population of only forty-five thousand, but its ruling family were generally a talented lot. They included passionate builders who have left a rich architectural legacy, a good businessman who built up the family fortunes to make them one of the richest of the German royal families, and astute politicians who ensured the survival of this tiny country right up to the end of the German monarchy in 1918. Schaumburg-Lippe avoided the fate of its much bigger neighbour, Hannover, of being swallowed up by Prussia. (See chart 1 in appendix E about the talented princes of Schaumburg-Lippe.)

But our day at Bückeburg started off with a minor setback. We arrived at the schloss to find that it can only be visited by guided tour and the first one was not due to start for two hours. In my experience guided tours are variable, depending on the knowledge and approach of the guide. They can be very good, but often they are just a rehearsed patter

with visitors herded from room to room on a timetable. A further difficulty for us is that, quite naturally, guided tours are usually in German.
But while we were deciding what to do, things looked up. The guide arrived for work early, some other visitors expressed interest, and it was
decided to put on an extra guided tour just for us. Within a very short
time, we were enjoying the best guided tour I have ever taken.

1. Bückeburg is a special place—a treasure house of history and art.

The reason why it was so good was that our guide (Oliver) was an
expert art historian who showed both great knowledge of and genuine
interest in the history of the schloss. He spoke good English, switching
languages to talk to both the English and the German visitors on his
tour. And, most importantly, there was no patter. Our guide not only

pointed out all the highlights of the schloss, but he also responded to our personal interests, talking to my husband about the history of the building and to me about the Schaumburg-Lippe family and the collection of portraits. He enthusiastically answered questions from all the visitors.

Schloss Bückeburg was built in phases between the fourteenth and the twentieth centuries. Over the generations, the family remodelled it or added new wings to meet the changing fashions of the day. In the sixteenth and seventeenth centuries, the original small castle was converted into a Renaissance palace; in the eighteenth century, parts of this were rebuilt in baroque style; and at the end of the nineteenth century, new wings were added in neobaroque style to create a grand entrance. Last to be built, on the cusp of World War I, was the mausoleum.

Our guided tour started in the sumptuous Renaissance palace created by Prince Ernst of Holstein-Schaumburg (1569–1622), who was one of the dynasty's most famous members and an important builder. (Holstein-Schaumburg was the family name before it became Schaumburg-Lippe.) Ernst succeeded in 1601 and transformed the schloss into one of the best known in Europe. He was the founder of the town of Bückeburg and left behind a wonderful legacy of two glorious rooms in the schloss, the chapel and the Golden Hall.

Like many princes of his time, Ernst travelled to Italy and was inspired by what he saw. He returned to transform the original chapel at Bückeburg (which dated from the Middle Ages) into a lavishly decorated work of art in the late Renaissance style. This is called mannerism and is characterised by elaborate and exaggerated decoration. The chapel is a visual feast of fresco paintings and carved lime (linden) wood covered in gold leaf. A golden pulpit hangs in front of the organ and above the altar, which is supported by two huge golden angels. At the other end of the chapel, the entire wall is covered by the ornate carved and gilded prince's pew. It does seem odd that all this flamboyance was created at a time when the Reformation was already affecting religious practices in Germany. Ernst's father had converted to

Lutheranism, which favoured a more austere and Spartan place of worship. The frescos in the chapel were whitewashed over just a few years after they were painted and only revealed on a restoration in the 1890s.

The chapel was under scaffolding when we were there, so we were not able to see it in its full glory. We did however see the Heavenly Gate (the entrance door) in the Golden Hall, another masterpiece created by Ernst which is considered one of the greatest achievements of German wood sculpture from its time.[2] It is the most famous thing in the schloss. In St Martin's Church in nearby Stadthagen, Ernst also created one of the most amazing artworks I have ever seen.

The Prince Ernst Mausoleum at Stadthagen

The town of Stadthagen was the main residence of the family before Prince Ernst of Holstein-Schaumburg moved this to Bückeburg in 1606. After the last ruling prince of Schaumburg-Lippe abdicated in 1918, the schloss at Stadthagen was confiscated by the state and it is now a tax office. It's open to visitors in the morning, but we were there in the afternoon. So instead, we went to see the mausoleum built by Prince Ernst in St Martin's Church.

We bought our tickets at the entrance to the church and a curator led us down the aisle and behind the altar, where she unlocked a small door. We had no idea what to expect, and the impact when we stepped inside was enormous. It is a breathtakingly beautiful place. This small, high, heptagonal (seven-sided) room at the back of St Martin's Church is flooded with light and full of energy. In the centre of the room there is a wonderful bronze-and-marble, three-tiered sculpture by Adriaen de Vries, who was the most famous sculptor in the mannerist style. It is of the resurrected Christ rising above the sleeping watchmen, and it contributes to the feeling of joy and hope that fills the room.

I read in the Bückeburg guidebook that if this room were in Florence or Venice, it would attract millions of visitors each year. I think this must be true. But here in Northern Germany we were the only two visitors; and so we stood there in awe, just the two of us with the curator.

Back in the chapel at Bückeburg, we were touched also to see a plainer and simpler memorial. Set into the floor in front of the altar are a number of metal crosses, smaller for children and larger for adults. They mark the family 'heart graves', where the hearts of members of the Schaumburg-Lippe family are buried. Their bodies were interred in the family mausoleum but their hearts were buried here, where it was thought they would be closest to God.

The White Hall is in the part of the schloss that is in the baroque style and houses a collection of family portraits. I enjoy looking at portraits and find them a great help in understanding family trees. For some reason particular ones stay in my mind, and at Bückeburg three stood out for me.

2. The Schaumberg-Lippe were a talented family—on the left Graf Wilhelm, who was the military genius of the family; on the right Prince Georg Wilhelm, a good businessman who built up the family fortunes.

The first was of the last reigning prince, Adolf II (1883–1936), who abdicated in 1918. My husband and I immediately christened his picture the Jaunty Prince because he is dressed in a bow tie with a flower in his buttonhole. He looks like a man-about-town ready for a night out. Adolf and his wife were killed in a plane crash in Mexico in 1936. The second was of Georg Wilhelm (1784–1860), who reigned for seventy-three years and was the longest-reigning prince. He was a good businessman who built up the family fortunes by clever investments in local industries such as mining and brickworks. There is a story about how, when a Rothschild from the banking dynasty came into a room full of German princes, they all stood up—except for the prince of Schaumburg-Lippe. The punch line was that this was because he was the only one who was not in debt to the Rothschilds.[3] Apparently Georg Wilhelm was also a miser and this is shown in his portrait, in which only one of the two candles in his candelabra is alight.[4]

The third portrait that immediately took my attention was of Graf Wilhelm (1724–1777), who was the military genius in the family. This portrait intrigued me because it is a copy of an original in St James's Palace in London that was painted by the English portrait painter Reynolds. To understand why an Englishman painted the portrait of a German prince, we have to go back to the unhappy marriage of Wilhelm's grandmother, Joanne Sophie (1673–1743).

She was married to Graf Friedrich Christian of Schaumburg-Lippe, whose portrait is also in the White Hall. It must have been a bad marriage for Joanne Sophie, because she left her husband and took her two sons to forge an independent career at the court of Hannover. There she became a great favourite of the elderly Electress Sophia of Hannover, who was heiress to the throne of Great Britain (Sophia's amazing life story is in *Schloss I*). Joanne Sophie was one of the courtiers who were walking with the electress in the gardens at Herrenhausen when Sophia suddenly collapsed and died in June 1714. We know exactly what happened because Joanne Sophie wrote a detailed letter to Sophia's niece afterwards describing the events in detail.[5] It is clear from this letter that Joanne Sophie was an intelligent and resourceful woman. She did everything she could to help the dying Sophia, supporting her on the ground in the heavy rain whilst sending for help and cutting open her corsets with a knife. When Sophia's son became George I of Great Britain a few weeks later, Joanne Sophie and her sons followed his court to live in England. There she remained a close friend of the royal family and was later given charge of the king's grand-children after his rift with his son.[6]

In 1722 Joanne Sophie's son Graf Albrecht Wolfgang of Schaum-burg-Lippe (1699–1743) cemented the family friendship when he mar-ried Margarethe Gertrud, known as Trudchen, who was the youngest of the three illegitimate daughters of George I by his long-term mis-tress Melusine von Schulenburg. It was Albrecht Wolfgang who rebuilt the east wing at Bückeburg in the baroque style after it was damaged by fire in the 1730s. He and Trudchen were the parents of Graf Wilhelm.

So Wilhelm was born and grew up in England. He became an En-glish field marshal and one of the most successful military commanders of his day, successfully defending Portugal from invasion in the Seven Years' War. He built the military fortress of Wilhelmstein on a man-made island on Lake Steinhude near Bückeburg to defend his princi-pality against aggressive neighbours. Our guide showed us the most extraordinary sketch with an early design for a submarine on Lake Steinhude, made for Wilhelm in the 1770s. In the days before steam power was invented, this submarine was intended to be rowed by oars!

The White Hall leads into the opulent Festival Hall, decorated in pink, gold, and white. This is twenty-four metres long and nine me-tres high and takes up the whole of the neobaroque right wing, which was added to the front of the schloss by Prince Georg II (1846–1911) at the end of the nineteenth century. It doubled the length of the schloss front. He also built two cavalier houses in the same grand style, one at each end of the enlarged front, to create an impressive entrance courtyard. A cavalier house was a supplementary building that usually housed the royal household. The royal family itself lived in the main schloss, and courtiers and guests in the cavalier house. The name prob-ably comes from cavalry, and these buildings may have originally been used for troops.

3. The opulent Festival Hall at Schloss Bückeburg.

The Festival Hall was the first part of the schloss to have central heating. Our guide told us that it is so large that when they held a party there, the central heating needed to be put on ten days beforehand to warm it up in time. Towards the end of our tour we walked down a beautiful Juliet balcony called the Trumpeter's Walk, which runs at a high level all the way around two sides of the inner schloss courtyard. This was much to the delight of my husband, who appreciated it as an impressive piece of engineering.

The guided tour at Bückeburg was a real highlight of our tour. So many things have stayed in my mind from it that I do not have room to write about here. The schloss is a treasure house of art, but it still retains some feeling of a family home, and this is partly because there are no museum displays or information boards. We were fortunate that our guide spoke good English because otherwise much of the content would have been inaccessible to us. After the tour I bought the English guidebook, which I highly recommend; it has interesting content and colourful diagrams and illustrations.

The Schaumburg-Lippe Family

The Schaumburg-Lippe family can trace their ancestry back to 1100 and Count Adolf I of Schaumburg, who is the first documented family member. In the Middle Ages, as counts of Holstein-Schaumburg, they had large land-holdings in the far north of Germany in Holstein, where they founded the cities of Lübeck and Kiel, as well as in the county of Schaumburg in Lower Saxony. By the middle of the fifteenth century however, almost all their ruling rights in Holstein had disappeared.

In 1647, after the death of the last count of Holstein-Schaumburg without an heir, the old county of Schaumburg split into two. The new state of Schaumburg-Lippe passed to a distant branch of the family, and Philip I became the first count of Schaumburg-Lippe. There would be five more counts, followed by four princes, before the German monarchy came to an end.

The first prince was Georg Wilhelm, who was promoted from count to prince in 1807, during the Napoleonic wars. He was smart enough to take Schaumburg-Lippe out of the Holy Roman Empire and into the new Confederation of the Rhine, which was sponsored by Napoleon, and the increase in title was his reward. A generation later his son, Adolf Georg, would prove equally astute politically when he threw in his lot with Prussia following the Seven Weeks' War of 1866. As a result, Schaumburg-Lippe kept its independence while other states were annexed by Prussia. When the new German Empire was proclaimed in 1871, following the Prussian victory in the Franco-Prussian war, Schaumburg-Lippe was a member state.

The last ruling prince of Schaumburg-Lippe was Adolf II. He abdicated his ruling rights in November 1918, when revolution shook Germany at the end of World War I.

After the end of the German monarchy in 1918, the family reached an agreement with the new Free State of Schaumburg-Lippe and retained the ownership of Schloss Bückeburg. The first sightseeing tours took place in 1925, so the family have been in the business of doing these for ninety years! The schloss suffered no damage in World War II, but at the end of the war was taken over by the British as the headquarters of the RAF (Royal Air Force). Inevitably there was pilfering, and our guide told us how things are still being returned; for example, some glassware came back recently at a reunion. When the family got the schloss back in the 1950s they resumed the sightseeing tours. They still own the schloss today.

Oldenburg

From Schaumburg-Lippe we drove north to see three schlösser in another of the historic principalities that lay in the present-day state of Lower Saxony. This was the grand duchy of Oldenburg, which stretched south from the coast of the North Sea. While there, we would come across several interesting characters from the family that ruled Oldenburg, including a duke who is always known by his initials and a deposed queen. We would also begin to unravel the thrilling story of how a German princess took over the throne of Russia. Our first schloss was in the capital city of the duchy, which is also called Oldenburg.

4. Schloss Oldenburg is a grand baroque building, painted in soft pale yellow with interesting carved stone detailing.

Schloss Oldenburg is a grand baroque building, painted in soft, pale yellow with interesting carved stone detailing. In front of the schloss is a large and attractive cobbled palace square, and here we were greeted by the statue of Duke Peter Friedrich Ludwig of Oldenburg, or PFL as he is always affectionately known. He is a well-known and respected figure here, and we would come across his name and image everywhere. For a duke who played such a large role in the duchy, his statue is quite modest and unassuming. Sculpted in bronze by Karl Gundelach in 1893, it has clean and uncluttered lines and looks modern in appearance. PFL is not shown in heroic mode, but simply standing on the plinth wearing his everyday clothes, which was apparently a trademark in all his portraits. It was much in contrast to the portraits of his ancestors that we would later see, in which they are dressed in magnificent state robes to show off their wealth and power.[7]

Chart 2 shows the family tree of PFL. He was not destined at his birth in 1755 to be the duke of Oldenburg. His father was a member of the Holstein-Gottorf family and the younger brother of Friedrich August, who was the reigning prince bishop of Lübeck. The prince bishop already had a son, born the year before in 1754, so it did not appear then that PFL would be his heir. By 1773 however, when Friedrich August also became duke of Oldenburg, it was clear that his son was mentally incapacitated and unfit to rule. When Friedrich August died in 1785 his son inherited the title of duke of Oldenburg in name, but his cousin PFL ruled the duchy as regent on his behalf. He proved an able administrator and was also a great benefactor to Oldenburg, founding hospitals, schools, and museums.[8] PFL ruled as regent for thirty-eight years before eventually becoming the duke in his own right on his cousin's death in 1823.

PFL was not as fortunate in his private life as in his public life. He himself would have a long life, dying in 1829 at the age of seventy-four, but many of his closest family members died young. Both his parents died in 1763 while he was still only a child. He also lost his wife after only four years of marriage. In 1781 he married the teenaged Princess

Friederike of Württemberg, who was the younger sister of the wife of Tsar Paul of Russia. Their marriage was a happy one and the couple's sons, Paul Friedrich August (August) and Peter Friedrich Georg (Georg), were born in 1783 and 1784 respectively. Later on our tour (at Schloss Eutin in Schleswig-Holstein), we would see a charming double portrait of them as little boys painted around 1787. The younger of the two is still in what was in those days the equivalent of nappies—a loose and open-bottomed dress with no underpants![9]

5. Duke Peter Friedrich Ludwig of Oldenburg is always affectionately known as PFL.

In the background of this double portrait, the painter has included an urn and a broken tree as symbols that the boys had already lost their mother. Friederike died in 1785, aged only twenty, after the stillbirth of her third child. PFL was inconsolable and never married again.[10] 'I know not what happiness is,' he wrote after his wife's death.[11] PFL's younger son Georg died from typhus at age twenty-nine, and he also lost three daughters-in-law (all wives of his elder son August).

While we were visiting Oldenburg, the town was celebrating the bicentenary of the schloss garden (1814–2014) with a series of events and a special exhibition at different venues across the town. One of the first things we saw was a huge banner draped down the front of the schloss advertising this. We were in for a surprise when we visited that part of the exhibition being held in the schloss. In the first room there was a large map of the UK on the floor and a video showing English gardens, including some that we know well, such as Stourhead in Wiltshire, near where I grew up. This is because the schloss garden that was created by PFL at Oldenburg was in the style of an English landscape garden, and Stourhead was the very first English landscape garden of them all, created in the 1740s.[12]

Towards the end of the eighteenth century, a craze swept across the courts of Germany as dukes and princes rushed to replace their gardens with these newly fashionable English landscape parks. We would come across these everywhere in Germany, and it would be the exception to find a schloss that still had the formal French baroque style of garden that had been fashionable before then. One wonderful example of this that does survive is the glorious Grosser Garten at Herrenhausen on the outskirts of Hannover city (see *Schloss I*). PFL was infected with this craze when he travelled to England in the 1770s, before his marriage to Friederike.

The new English style of landscape gardening replaced formal paths and geometric flower beds with the more natural look of sweeping lawns, meadows, lakes, and belts of trees. The idea was to reproduce pictures from landscape paintings. It was an idealised view of the countryside where sheep graze on the lawns and the view is dotted with garden follies and classical temples. Of course this is not a natural landscape at all, and everything in it was contrived by man. The trees were carefully planted to create vistas, the river diverted, and the lake dug out by hand. Even the sheep were orchestrated, being kept away

The Holstein-Gottorf Family

The Schleswig-Holstein-Gottorf family (or Holstein-Gottorf for short) were a branch of the extended royal house of Oldenburg. The house had numerous branches, and chart 3 shows (in simplified form) those that are included in this book. Even within the Holstein-Gottorf family there were two different lines—a senior line who were the dukes of Holstein-Gottorf, and a junior line. It was the junior line that became dukes of Oldenburg in 1773.

The 1773 Treaty of Tsarskoye Selo was an attempt to resolve the knotty problem of the disputed territories of Schleswig and Holstein in the Jutland peninsula. In Russia, Catherine the Great's son and heir, Grand Duke Paul, was also the duke of Holstein-Gottorf, which title he had inherited from his father. In return for Russia renouncing Paul's rights to Schleswig and Holstein in favour of the Danish crown, Denmark ceded Oldenburg and Delmenhorst to Russia. These were then given to the junior line of the Holstein-Gottorf family, who were closely related to the Russian royal family (see chart 4). The two were then incorporated into the new duchy of Oldenburg, which was recognised as a sovereign state within the Holy Roman Empire.

Friedrich August, who became the first duke of Oldenburg under the new arrangements, was already the ruler of a small church state some distance away in Holstein, called the Prince Bishopric of Lübeck (the prefix 'prince' means simply that the ruler was of royal status). Although an ecclesiastical state the prince bishopric was ruled by secular princes, who were originally elected to the role. By the time Friedrich August succeeded his elder brother in 1750 however, it had long been a sinecure of the Holstein-Gottorf family. In 1803 the little church state was secularised as the principality of Lübeck and subsumed into the duchy of Oldenburg.

During the Napoleonic Wars, France annexed the duchy of Oldenburg and the ducal family had to flee into exile. They returned at the end of the wars and in 1815, at the Congress of Vienna, Oldenburg was promoted to a grand duchy. PFL refused to use the title of grand duke however, as a protest, since he believed that the congress had not treated him well enough. The grand duchy of Oldenburg survived until the end of the German monarchy in 1918.

from the house by an invisible 'ha-ha' (a deep ditch they could not cross). These gardens, which in their day were ultramodern, have stood the test of time and many survive today. Perhaps this is due not only to their beauty, but also to their practicality. This is a relatively low-maintenance style of gardening, needing fewer gardeners.

The last grand duke of Oldenburg, Friedrich August, was the great-grandson of PFL. He abdicated his rights in November 1918 after revolutionaries forced him to raise the red flag over Schloss Oldenburg. The schloss was confiscated and became the property of the new Free State of Oldenburg. Today it houses a museum of the history of Oldenburg right up to the present day. We visited this, but sadly there was little information in English. It was a relief to find a friendly museum attendant who spoke some English, and also several helpful maps, charts, and family trees, which are fairly easy to understand in any language. I vividly remember a colourful stained-glass window with portraits of PFL and his three grand duke successors.

The museum includes the main rooms of the schloss from its days as a ducal residence. I particularly liked the elegant but strangely named Marble Ballroom (strange because there is no marble in it). One of the few signs in English told us that this was where PFL's eldest granddaughter Amalie was married in 1836. In our next schloss we would find out more about Amalie, who was the first queen of Greece.

Rastede Palais

We stopped at the tourist information office in the pleasant and leafy country town of Rastede, just a few miles north of Oldenburg, to enquire about visiting their schloss. Here we were told that Rastede Schloss is still owned by the Oldenburg family but that it is not open to the public. Our journey might have been wasted had we not got chatting to the helpful assistant who had recently returned from a motorbike holiday in the English West Country and was full of the joys of Devon lanes and English bed-and-breakfast. He pointed out that there are two Oldenburg palaces in Rastede and suggested that we might want to visit Rastede Palais instead. We are very glad he did so; otherwise we would have missed this charming small schloss.

6. Rastede Palais was the much-loved childhood summer home of Amalie of Oldenburg, later queen of Greece.

Rastede Palais was the childhood summer home of Princess Amalie of Oldenburg, later Queen Amalie of Greece. Amalie was the princess with three mothers. Her father was Duke August of Oldenburg, the eldest of the two sons of PFL. He married three times and lost all his wives young as a result of childbirth (see chart 2). He married first Adelheid of Anhalt Bernburg in 1817, and Amalie was their eldest child born the following year. A second daughter followed in 1820, but Adelheid never recovered from this birth and died, aged twenty, a few weeks later. So Amalie lost her own mother before she was two years old. Five years later August was married to Ida of Anhalt Bernburg, who was the younger sister of his first wife. Perhaps they had become close as a result of their joint bereavement, or Ida may have been a devoted aunt for the two little motherless Oldenburg princesses. Poor Ida had already lost two of her three sisters to childbirth and seemed to have a premonition that the same would happen to her.[13] Sadly she was right. She never properly recovered from the birth of her son (the future Grand Duke Peter), and she died in 1828, aged twenty-four. Amalie lost her first stepmother before she was ten years old.

Her father married for a third time just three years later, this time to Princess Cecilie of Sweden. Perhaps he was a man who could not do without the support and companionship of a wife, or perhaps he felt that a single son was not enough and that there must be at least one more, as the 'spare'. By the time of this marriage he had succeeded his father to become the first grand duke of Oldenburg, so Cecilie was the first grand duchess. Two sons were born to the couple quite quickly, in 1834 and 1836, but both died when they were around a year old. A third son, Elimar, was born in 1844, but this time Cecilie did not survive the birth and died a few days later, aged 36.

The tragic history of the early deaths of all three wives of Grand Duke August really brought home the huge risks to women in the nineteenth century from childbirth. In the middle of the century (the time by which record keeping had become reliable), the statistics show death rates in England and Wales at almost five per cent, or one in twenty women.[14] The three big killers were infection, haemorrhage, and convulsions (eclampsia), and the causes and treatment of these were not yet understood. In an age when we do not expect anyone whom we know to die in childbirth, it is hard to imagine the real terror that must have gripped young women as they approached their confinements. One might say that in Oldenburg, three young women died in the interests of producing heirs to carry on the line.

As a child Amalie must surely have felt the lack of a mother, and the death of two baby brothers would also have affected her. The curator at Rastede Palais told us that Amalie had a sad and unfulfilled life, but that the Palais was the childhood home she loved and the place where she had been happy.

7. Amalie has been called the princess with three mothers, because all of her father's three wives died young as a result of childbirth.

Rastede Palais is a small building set back in the trees on the other side of the road to the main schloss. Rastede Schloss was the summer residence of PFL, and he built Rastede Palais for his eldest son and family in the early 1820s. Prints from that time show the Palais as a single-story building in elegant classical style with a grand central portico and entrance. It is not so attractive to look at today; in the 1880s Amalie's brother, Grand Duke Peter, added an extra story giving it an unbalanced and clumsy appearance.

It was however a most enjoyable place to visit. Despite now being a museum it retains a cosy feel and happy atmosphere, and it was easy to picture it as a family home. We were the only visitors that afternoon and wandered contentedly around the rather unkempt grounds. Inside there is a gallery of modern art downstairs and an exhibition of the history of Rastede as an Oldenburg summer residence on the first floor. Everything was in German only, but the curator was very welcoming and responded to our interest. With the help of her halting English, we were able to piece together some of Amalie's story.

Amalie of Oldenburg married King Otto of Greece on 22 December 1836 in the Marble Ballroom at Schloss Oldenburg. Her new husband was the second son of King Ludwig I of Bavaria and had been king of Greece since he was sixteen. Otto is the forgotten king of Greece but he reigned for thirty years from 1832, after Greece became independent of the Ottoman Empire. The Great Powers (Britain, France, and Russia) decided that the new country should be a kingdom and approached King Ludwig, who accepted the throne on behalf of his son. In 1835, when he was twenty, Otto reached his majority and assumed full powers. It was now imperative that he get married and father an heir as soon as possible, and the following year he set out for Germany to find a bride. His choice fell on seventeen-year-old Amalie who, he wrote to his father, was 'a vision of grace, beautiful in every way.'[15] But he was not then in love. Otto was marrying to order, and in the same letter he told his father that as he had only met his fiancé only a few days before, he was 'not perturbed that my courtship has not begun with an impetuous passion.'[16]

I did not find a firsthand account of Amalie's feelings at the time of her engagement. But Otto was tall (over six feet) and, judging by his portraits, extremely good looking. As the king of a faraway and exotic country, he must have seemed a romantic figure, so perhaps she was swept off her feet. What does seem clear is that it became a very happy marriage. In her letters home from Greece to her father in Oldenburg, Amalie writes how she adores her husband and how his love for her is very touching. In a letter of November 1841 she tells how, when she returned to Greece from a trip to Germany, Otto met her ship and rushed to her cabin for a private reunion before the official greeting.[17]

Otto and Amalie were king and queen of Greece for the next twenty-six years. They loved their new country and tried hard, wearing Greek costume and touring the country, but they never achieved much popularity among their subjects. Otto was hard of hearing and had a slight stammer; he was accused of being slow of understanding and not able to see the wood for the trees.[18] He was not the sort of charismatic and decisive ruler that the Greeks might have warmed to. Amalie on the other hand, was considered to be too clever, dominant, and interfering. A report back to the British Foreign Office complained that

the King reads all documents placed before him but signs none, whereas the Queen, when Regent, reads none but signs all.[19]

8. King Otto and Queen Amalie wearing Greek costume in the cathedral at Athens; they never achieved much popularity among their subjects.

There were huge expectations on the couple to produce an heir to the throne, but it never happened. There was only ever one mention of a possible pregnancy, in a letter from Otto to his father in June 1837, but if that was the case it must have ended in a miscarriage[20]. Amalie's letters over the years chart her growing despair at her failure to have a child. In November 1839, after three years of marriage, she writes to her father that she is happy and content and is convinced that her wish to have children will come true in the following year.[21] Four years later she sees it as the hand of providence and writes on 1 January 1844, in a New Year's letter to her father-in-law

> I thank God for having given me such a husband whom I can love and respect; and that I am in a land which, in spite of a thousand drawbacks, I can still love;...The only thing lacking is children; and I know God will send them to me, in His own time.[22]

But by 1848, after twelve years of marriage, the tone of her letters is shrill. She feels blamed for the lack of children and is at pains to stress that it cannot be her fault because she has tried everything, consulted all the doctors, and been through all their cures, however unpleasant. Apparently one suggested remedy to get a son was to mix gunpowder into Otto's food![23] It is impossible to say how much difference a child would have made to their popularity, but an heir born in Greece and brought up in the Orthodox religion would surely have helped the popularity of the new dynasty.

The failure to conceive must also have been a personal tragedy for the couple, and one wonders how it affected their relationship. It is suggested that Otto fathered a son before his marriage, with a girl from a nomadic group of Greek mountain shepherds, and that their descendants still live in Athens.[24] There have also been rumours that he was unfaithful to Amalie with the notorious Jane Digby, who arrived to live in Athens at the end of 1842.

Born an English aristocrat, Jane had already left behind two divorced husbands, three abandoned children, and several lovers, one of whom was Otto's father, King Ludwig I of Bavaria, who was probably the father of her daughter Bertha.[25] Jane would live in Athens on and off for the next decade, first with her third husband, the Greek Count Spiros Theotoky (who was an aide-de-camp to King Otto), and then with her next lover, Greek Colonel Xristodolous Hadji-Petros. Jane got on well with Otto, just as she had with his father, but both their biographers denied a love affair.[26] However, she seems to have aroused feelings of jealousy and insecurity in Amalie. Jane's biographer paints a picture of Amalie as a frustrated and bitter woman who viewed Jane as a rival and tried to get her ostracised from Athenian society.[27] To some extent this rings true when one considers that by 1852, when Jane began her affair with Hadji-Petros, Amalie was in her mid-thirties, still barren and unpopular in her adopted country.

King Otto and Queen Amalie were deposed in a bloodless coup in October 1862 while they were on a trip to the south of the country. Otto never actually abdicated, but no one took much notice of this. The couple returned quietly to Bavaria and settled in the schloss at Bamberg. Neither of them lived long, both dying in their fifties. When Otto went first from measles in 1867, Amalie wrote to her father-in-law,

In Otho I lost all. For thirty years he was the most beloved, true, and gentle husband to me. What have we not been through together—how every ordeal bound us closer! We were absolutely dependant on each other.[28]

Without Otto, Amalie lost her reason for living and quickly became an old woman, indulging her passion for sweet things and putting on weight.[29] She died in 1875, aged fifty-seven. Today Otto and Amalie are the forgotten king and queen of Greece, and I found it difficult to find material on them in English. There is only one biography of Otto, written in 1939. His only lasting memorial is the foundation of Athens as the capital of Greece.

In the small shop at Rastede Palais, my husband noticed a flyer for a nearby castle called Schloss Jever. Although the leaflet was in German it was most intriguing because it included a picture of Catherine the Great. What was the picture of the famous Russian empress doing in a leaflet advertising a schloss in Lower Saxony? We went to Jever to find out.

The Fate of German Princesses in the Royal Marriage Market

Whenever one of Europe's royal houses was looking for a bride, one or more German princesses were sure to be in the running. With multiple royal families there were simply more princesses to choose from than in any other country, and this was what made Germany the royal marriage market. A principality might be tiny and the ruling family poor, but its daughters were of royal blood and therefore eligible. German princesses were selected to become queens and empresses and fulfil the greatest roles in the society of their day. But their personal lives were frequently unhappy, and their fates could be tragic.

When a bride was being selected, each candidate's qualifications would be carefully considered, including her age, character, family history, and whether she was likely to be a good 'breeder'. The bridegroom's personal characteristics were not considered so important, provided he had a good position. When Caroline Mathilde of Great Britain was shipped off to marry the king of Denmark in 1766, aged fifteen, her husband was known to be deranged and sometimes violent (see Celle in Schloss I).

Princesses were a commodity whose marriages were arranged to further family interests; to cement diplomatic alliances, establish rights of inheritance, and protect the families' bloodlines. There was little room for romantic love or courtship on the royal marriage market, and couples would often hardly know each other before the wedding. Princes might be allowed some say in the selection of a bride, as when Catherine the Great of Russia invited the three teenaged princesses of Saxe-Coburg to St Petersburg in 1795 on inspection for her second grandson, Constantine. Princesses more rarely had a choice; the Saxe-Coburg family were delighted with the prospect of being connected to the powerful and prestigious Russian court, and fourteen-year-old Juliane (who was the choice) was expected to say yes. The marriage was deeply unhappy, and Juliane escaped from her husband and his country as soon as she could.

The practice of marrying within a narrow circle meant that most of Europe's royal families were related, and marriages between cousins were *frequent. This could lead to inbreeding and the spread of inherited disease. The granddaughters of Queen Victoria carried haemophilia into the royal families of Russia and Spain, where it would bring tragedy and be a factor in the collapse of these thrones.*

Once she was married, the role of a princess was to secure the succession into the next generation by producing sons as quickly as possible. It was a rare example when Queen Victoria wrote to her eldest daughter, who was just married, urging her to wait a year before getting pregnant. Princesses who found themselves barren, like Amalie of Greece, came under enormous pressure. Those who were fertile faced the risks of childbirth and the wear and tear of frequent pregnancies. Queen Luise of Prussia died at thirty-four, worn out by producing ten children in fifteen years. Her mother, Friederike of Hesse-Darmstadt, had died at twenty-nine after having ten in thirteen years.

Jever

The small town of Jever (population fourteen thousand) is the capital of the district of Friesland, which borders the North Sea coast in Lower Saxony. Hundreds of years ago Jever was an important port, but changes in the land pattern mean that it is now well inland. In Germany the town is most well-known for the popular brand of beer called Jever, which is brewed there.

The schloss dates back to the fifteenth century and is painted in a warm pink colour. We had already noticed that German schlösser are often painted in vibrant colours, and where these are a particular feature I will try to describe the colours, as the illustrations in this book are in black-and-white. But at Jever the most prominent feature is the sixty-seven-metre-high round central tower, which was built in the 1730s. This dwarfs the front of the schloss and takes up much of the space in the small internal courtyard.

Jever was once the capital of a small, independent principality ruled by the lords of Jeverland. The last of the line was Maria of Jever

(1500–1575), who was so important in local history that even today the town is sometimes known as Marienstadt, or Maria City. But Maria never married, and when she died she left her state to a branch of the Oldenburg family. When they died out too, nearly a hundred years later in 1667, it was inherited by a nephew of the last Oldenburg lord of Jever (the son of his sister who had married a prince of Anhalt-Zerbst). So Jever passed to the Anhalt-Zerbst family who held it until 1793. This is the reason why the portrait of Catherine the Great of Russia (or in German, Katharina der Grosse) was in the schloss flyer and also greeted us on a large banner outside the schloss gates. It is because Catherine was born Princess Sophie Friederike Auguste of Anhalt-Zerbst, and she once owned the schloss.

9. A central tower, sixty-seven metres tall, dwarfs the front of the schloss at Jever.

Anhalt-Zerbst was another of the patchwork of independent states that then made up Germany. It was also very small, so the acquisition of Jeverland must have added considerably to its wealth. This demonstrated for us the importance of arranged marriages in securing inheritance rights through the female line. The marriage of an Oldenburg princess brought Jeverland into the Anhalt-Zerbst family in 1667. The marriage of her descendant Sophie would take it into the Russian royal family when the Anhalt-Zerbst line died out in turn in 1793.

An exhibition at Schloss Jever called *Remote Rulers* covers aspects of life in the court, the town, and the country during the years that it was ruled by the Anhalt-Zerbst family. Zerbst is nearly 250 miles away (in the present-day state of Saxony-Anhalt), which was a considerable distance in those days. The family were absentee landlords and only visited Jever occasionally for a few weeks in summer. The tenants who normally lived in the schloss would be forced to vacate temporarily so it could be prepared for the family. And they would bring their own furniture, tapestries, and other household goods with them.

The most memorable room in the schloss is the Princely Gallery on the first floor, which has been a museum open to the public since the 1920s. It is a long, narrow room that houses portraits of the rulers of Jeverland across the centuries. They include a portrait of Catherine, but this is a very different one to that which we had already seen in the flyer and on the banner outside the gate. That was painted in 1794, the year after Catherine inherited Jeverland from her brother, and it was a personal gift from the empress to the schloss where it has hung ever since. It shows the mature and confident empress in a regal stance. The portrait in the gallery dates from fifty years earlier and shows the young Sophie of Anhalt-Zerbst at the time of her betrothal to the heir to the Russian throne. A little booklet in English, which is a guide to the Princely Gallery, says that this portrait comes close to the description that Catherine's mother gave of her at the time:

> Her head was completely uncovered, except for a ribbon; her hair was unpowdered, no jewellery, only her large earrings and the ribbon. She was a little pale and I can say she appeared absolutely wonderful to me.[30]

When Sophie was born on 21 April 1729 she was just another princess from one of many small German states, and no one could have foretold that she would become the reigning empress of Russia. Her father, Prince Christian-August of Anhalt-Zerbst, was a career soldier in the Prussian army; her mother was Princess Johanna Elizabeth of Holstein-Gottorf. Johanna was much younger than her husband and a cut above him socially. She was dissatisfied with her husband, her life as an officer's wife, and the sex of her first child.[31] She had wanted Sophie to be a boy. She never showed much affection to her daughter, and the young Sophie soon learned to rely on her own resources and keep her own counsel. These were qualities that would stand her in good stead during her difficult years at the Russian court before she became empress.

At fourteen years old, Sophie was considering a proposal of marriage from her uncle (her mother's brother) when an invitation arrived from Tsarina Elizabeth to visit the Russian court with her mother on approval as a possible bride for Elizabeth's heir, Grand Duke Peter. Elizabeth was the daughter of Tsar Peter the Great and had seized the Russian throne three years earlier. She never made a dynastic marriage but she was well aware of the need to secure the succession and had already brought her young nephew (the son of her dead sister Anna) to Russia, renamed him Grand Duke Peter, and declared him as her successor. He was a year older than Sophie. But a single heir could sicken and die at any time, so that Elizabeth was anxious for Peter to marry as soon as possible and father children. She probably picked Sophie as his bride for sentimental reasons.[32] Elizabeth had once been engaged to another of Johanna's brothers, but he had died of smallpox before the wedding.

Sophie and her mother arrived at the Russian court in February 1744. In June she was betrothed to Peter and became Grand Duchess Ekaterina Alexeevna (Catherine). Normally an arranged marriage would then have taken place immediately, but the new grand duchess had to wait until August 1745 for her wedding. The reason for the delay was the opinion of the doctors that Peter was still sexually immature and could not yet father a child.[33] During all these months at the Russian court she was under constant observation by courtiers who were only too willing to carry tales to the tsarina. Catherine was well aware that she could be sent packing by Elizabeth at any time. She wasn't helped by the insensitive behaviour of her mother, who was soon in Elizabeth's bad books.

But Catherine was ambitious and, despite her personal dislike of the grand duke, determined to seize her opportunity. She kept her head, tried to please everybody, and wrote in her memoirs,

> I treated everyone as best I could and made it my task to earn the friendship or at least to lessen the enmity of those whom I suspected of being evilly disposed towards me....I showed great respect to my mother, and unlimited obedience to the Empress, the greatest consideration for the Grand Duke, and I sought with the greatest earnestness the public's affection.[34]

Once married, Catherine's position was more secure, but not much. Both bride and groom were very young and sexually inexperienced, and they did not much like each other. Their marriage would not be consummated for eight years. As the months and years went by with no sign of a baby, Elizabeth grew increasingly frustrated and angry; she put most of the blame on Catherine. The deadlock was resolved only after a young widow was hired to instruct Peter in how to make love and Catherine was encouraged to take a lover. Her son, Pavel Petrovich, the future Tsar Paul, was born on 20 September 1754. From her memoirs it was clear that Catherine was sleeping with both her husband and her lover (Sergei Saltykov) when she fell pregnant, and the possibility that Paul was illegitimate was the reason why the memoirs were kept secret by her successors.[35] The verdict of many historians, based on their similar appearances and characters, is that he was probably Peter's son.

Catherine was pregnant with her third child (fathered by her current lover Grigori Orlov) when Elizabeth died on Christmas Day 1761, and Peter became tsar. This was the most dangerous time of all for her. She and Peter were estranged, and he announced his intention to divorce her and marry his mistress. She could not pass her child off as her husband's and had to keep the pregnancy a secret. When she went into labour in April 1762, one of her faithful servants set fire to his own home to create a diversion. While Peter and the court rushed off to watch the fire, Catherine's son Alexis Bobrinsky was born and smuggled out of the palace.[36]

On 28 June that year, with the support of the regiments of Guards, organised by Grigori Orlov and his brothers, Catherine usurped her husband's throne. The coup was not contested, and no blood was shed apart from Peter's. He was killed in a scuffle with the men guarding him a few days later. Catherine had not ordered this, but there is no doubt that it was convenient for her. She would be the ruler of Russia for the next thirty-four years.

It seems extraordinary to us that Catherine should have been accepted as tsarina when she was not related by blood to previous tsars, or even Russian. But she was not the first female ruler to come to power as the result of a military coup; she was following the example of both her mother-in-law Elizabeth and Elizabeth's mother Ekaterina I. There was no rule in Russia that the throne must automatically pass from father to son or the nearest heir. After he had disinherited and killed his son, Peter the Great had issued the Law of Succession to the Throne in 1722, which provided that each Russian ruler was free to name his or her successor. Catherine felt that she was clearly so much better suited than her husband, Peter, and may have hoped that Elizabeth would nominate her in his place. There were many at court who thought that Catherine should only have ruled as regent until her son came of age, but her ambition meant that she could not pass up the opportunity for absolute power. She wrote in her memoirs that on the eve of her wedding.

My heart did not foresee great happiness; ambition alone sustained me. At the bottom of my soul I had something, I know not what, that never for a single moment let me doubt that sooner or later I would succeed in becoming the sovereign Empress of Russia in my own right[37].

10. Catherine the Great was born the princess of an insignificant German duchy, but used her body and her brains to become ruler of the vast Russian empire.

The lordship of Jever came to the Russian royal family in 1793, when the male line of Anhalt-Zerbst came to an end and Catherine inherited it from her last surviving brother. During the Napoleonic Wars the little territory was invaded by the French army, and under the Tilsit Peace Treaty of 1807, Tsar Alexander I (Catherine's grandson) signed it over to the new kingdom of Holland, which was ruled by Napoleon's brother, Louis Bonaparte. After Napoleon's defeat it reverted, and the tsar appointed his cousin, Duke Peter Friedrich Ludwig (PFL) as administrator of the territory. A few years later it became part of the grand duchy of Oldenburg, where it remained until the end of the monarchy in 1918.

On the wall just outside the gates there is a small plaque, almost hidden by ivy, which records the actions of some citizens of Jever as World War II was coming to an end. As the Allied armies advanced across Germany, a crowd gathered outside the schloss on 3 May 1945. Fearing destruction and loss of life, they risked their own lives to disarm the Nazis and hoist the white flag over the schloss tower. The plaque was put up fifty years later, in 1995.

11. A plaque commemorates events at Schloss Jever on 3 May 1945, at the end of World War II.

3

SCHLESWIG-HOLSTEIN AND ITS DUCAL FAMILIES

From Lower Saxony we travelled to the most northern of the sixteen German länder, the state of Schleswig-Holstein. In the middle of the nineteenth century this area, then the duchies of Schleswig and Holstein, was the subject of a complicated international crisis involving the Great Powers of the day. It led to one of the famous and best-used quotes in history when British Prime Minister Palmerston said,

> Only three people have ever really understood the Schleswig-Holstein business—the Prince Consort, who is dead—a German professor, who has gone mad—and I, who have forgotten all about it.

Palmerston was referring to the treaties, succession laws, and constitutional matters that made the issue so complex in international law and led to two wars over the duchies in the mid-nineteenth century before they were eventually annexed by Prussia. But in essence the issue was simple. The duchies were the border between Denmark and Germany, and both countries claimed them. Not surprisingly, the tussle over the duchies led to great bitterness between the Danes,

Prussians, and Schleswig-Holsteiners, and it split the loyalties of Europe's royal families. From our visits we would find out more about the Schleswig-Holstein question and the divisions and rivalries it caused. But first we were off to the ancestral home of the Holstein-Gottorf family, where we would come across one small boy who lay claim to the thrones of Sweden and Russia.

Eutin

Schloss Eutin was the residence of the rulers of a small church state called the Prince Bishopric of Lübeck (see Oldenburg in chapter 2). It was completely redesigned and rebuilt by Christian August of Holstein-Gottorf after he became the prince bishop in 1705. By this time the title of prince bishop had become hereditary, and the schloss was the main residence of the family until Peter Friedrich Ludwig (PFL) moved this to the schloss in Oldenburg city in 1803, after they had become dukes of Oldenburg.

PFL has been called the 'father of Eutin'.[38] From 1785 he administered the prince bishopric on behalf of his incapacitated cousin, and during these years Eutin had a golden age. PFL invited scholars, poets, and painters to the small town, and this is the reason why it is still today sometimes referred to as the Weimar of the North.[39] They included the painter Johann Heinrich Wilhelm Tischbein, whom PFL met in Italy and who was court painter in Eutin from 1809 until his death in 1829, and also the poet, Johann Heinrich Voss, who worked at Eutin from 1782 to 1802. Voss wrote that Eutin was 'lovely for the eye, captivating for the heart.'[40]

The schloss is in a glorious location in the area known as Holstein's Switzerland. It is built on a small promontory into the Grosser Eutiner See (Lake Eutin) and surrounded by a moat. Everywhere you look, the schloss is set against a backdrop of greenery and water. The building itself is simply stunning, with beautiful red brickwork on the outside walls and painted a warm apricot in the interior courtyard. It was a sunny day and with the café tables in the courtyard, a gentle fountain playing in the centre, and greenery growing up the glowing apricot coloured walls, we felt that we could almost be in the Mediterranean. Eutin rapidly became my favourite schloss in Schleswig-Holstein.

12. Schloss Eutin is a stunning building set in a beautiful area known as Holstein's Switzerland.

The schloss was the location for the first meeting of Princess Sophie of Anhalt-Zerbst (later Catherine the Great) and her future husband, when they were aged ten and eleven respectively. This was before he was taken to Russia by his aunt, Tsarina Elizabeth, to be renamed Grand Duke Peter and become her heir. He was still at that time Duke Karl Peter Ulrich of Holstein-Gottorf and the ward of his cousin, the prince bishop of Lübeck. The prince bishop was also Catherine's uncle (the brother of her mother Johanna of Holstein-Gottorf), so the two children were quite closely related (please see chart 4 for the family connection).

In her memoirs, Catherine was at pains to paint her husband in a very poor light. For example, regarding this first meeting at Eutin in 1739, she wrote that Peter 'already showed signs of his attraction to wine and his reluctance towards anything that was in any way difficult'.[41]

But Catherine rewrote and amended her memoirs after the event, and she was always concerned to justify her seizure of the throne on the grounds that Peter would have made a hopeless tsar. Her biographers suggest that although he was not as talented as she was, Peter was more intelligent and cultured than Catherine gave him credit for. One has suggested that his main problem was a lack of empathy (the inability to understand the effect of actions and words on others), which was a legacy from his unloved and isolated childhood.[42]

Peter was the son of Duke Karl Friedrich of Holstein-Gottorf and Anna Petrovna of Russia. Karl Friedrich's mother was the sister of the childless king of Sweden, and he was brought up at the Swedish court in the expectation of succeeding his uncle. When this did not happen, he decamped to the court of Peter the Great in St Petersburg, where he married the tsar's eldest daughter Anna (the sister of Tsarina Elizabeth). Their only child, Karl Peter Ulrich of Holstein-Gottorf, was born in 1728; Anna died just months later from consumption. Duke Karl Friedrich did not have much time for his son, who was brought up by tutors and military instructors without much affection and with no family life or friends of his own age. He was backward, shy and lonely, and frequently ill.

Peter was a child with huge expectations in life, which he was incapable of living up to. As well as being duke of Holstein-Gottorf after his father's death, he had a good claim to the Swedish throne through his paternal grandmother and to the Russian throne through his mother (see chart 5 for how these claims arose). Another of Catherine's biographers thinks that he would have made a good army officer, and this is a career that he probably would have enjoyed.[43] After he was taken to Russia as a fourteen-year-old and declared to be the future tsar, he only ever wanted to go back to Holstein and drill his soldiers. This was his plea to his wife Catherine after she deposed him. But, even if he had not been murdered, it is unlikely that she would have agreed to this, for the same reason that she later signed away her son's rights to Schleswig-Holstein—she did not want a rival claimant to the Russian throne with a power base in a German duchy.

When Karl Peter Ulrich of Holstein-Gottorf became Grand Duke Peter of Russia, he had to give up his claim to the Swedish throne. But Tsarina Elizabeth chose another member of the Holstein-Gottorf family to take this over—Catherine's uncle (and Johanna's brother) Adolf Friedrich; he became king of Sweden in 1751. So, through the claims of one small boy (Karl Peter Ulrich), the Holstein-Gottorf family took over the thrones of both Sweden and Russia. They occupied the Swedish throne until 1818, and (assuming that her husband was the father of Catherine's son Paul) all the remaining tsars of Russia until the 1917 revolution were descendants of the house of Holstein-Gottorf.

Schloss Eutin is a wonderful place to visit—it has an interesting history, a good English guide book, and the buildings are beautiful. If you are not able to visit but would like a glimpse, buy the film *Cabaret* with Liza Minnelli. Eutin stars as the country home of the degenerate baron who takes Sally Bowles and her boyfriend there and sleeps with them both. Watch for the scene where the baron's vintage car pulls up in the schloss courtyard.

13. Eutin is set against a backdrop of greenery and water.

What was most memorable for me was the amazing collection of royal portraits at the schloss. We were particularly lucky; in addition to the permanent exhibition of these, there was a special exhibition of many more while we were there. We were told that the current duchess of Oldenburg had arranged for portraits from all the Oldenburg schlösser to be brought to Eutin, where they were being catalogued by a professor from Oldenburg University.

There were portraits of all the members of the Oldenburg family, including PFL and his two sons as children; the three wives of Duke August, who all died in childbirth; and Queen Amalie, both as a child and as queen in Greek costume. Here too were portraits of the Holstein-Gottorf family before they became dukes of Oldenburg. We saw Catherine and Peter; her parents and grandparents; even the fiancé of Tsarina Elizabeth, who died before their wedding; and the young uncle who had wanted to marry the fourteen-year-old Catherine before she went to Russia. Through the family's connections there were portraits of the Swedish royal family and dozens of the Russians, from the time of Anna and Elizabeth (the two daughters of Peter the Great) down to the last tsar and tsarina, Nicholas and Alexandra.

I had never before seen a portrait of Grand Duchess Natalia Alexeyevna, the first wife of Catherine's son Paul, who died in childbirth in 1776 after an agonising five-day labour. A postmortem revealed a bone deformity, which meant that the birth canal was too narrow and she could never have delivered a live child.[44] Paul was devastated by her death, but Catherine could not allow him to grieve for long. Like her mother-in-law, Elizabeth, she was desperate for an heir in the next generation to secure the succession. So she had Natalia's desk broken into and then forced her son to read the letters that showed that his wife had been conducting an affair with his friend.[45] Within five months of his first wife's death, Paul was married again. His second wife would eventually give him four sons and six daughters.

The collection included a charming portrait of his fourth daughter, Grand Duchess Ekaterina Paulowna, wearing a white dress and a huge white bonnet trimmed with ostrich feathers. At Schloss Eutin I heard the story of how she came to marry Duke Georg of Oldenburg (the younger son of PFL) in 1809 (see chart 4). By this time Emperor Napoleon I of France, who also needed an heir, had decided to divorce his childless wife Josephine and marry again. He wanted to make a dynastic marriage this time around and suggested to Tsar Alexander I that his sister, Ekaterina, would be suitable for the role. Her family were horrified, and Ekaterina's mother immediately arranged a marriage for her with her second cousin Georg. He was told to come to Russia pronto and propose. Napoleon married Archduchess Marie Louise of Austria a few months later.

After the end of the monarchy in 1918, Schloss Eutin remained in the family ownership and parts were opened to the public as a museum. But during and after World War II, it suffered considerable damage when it was used first by the German army and then to house refugees fleeing from the Soviet zone of occupation, and as an old people's home. Restoration work was undertaken in the 1950s, but by the 1980s further extensive and costly work was required. In 1992 the schloss and its contents were transferred by the family to a newly established trust, the Stiftung Schloss Eutin, backed by central and state government money. This enabled the complete restoration of the schloss, which was officially reopened in 2006. The result is a triumph.

Kiel

In Schleswig-Holstein we stayed in Kiel, which in the dukes' time was the capital of Holstein and is now the capital of the federal state of Schleswig-Holstein. Situated on the Kiel Fjord at the base of the Jutland peninsula, Kiel commands the entrance to the Baltic Sea and has a strong maritime history. Known as the Sailing City, it is host each June to the famous Kiel Week, which is the largest sailing event in the world. This has been held every year since 1882, except for interruptions during the two world wars.

Kiel played an important role in the build-up of the German navy in the last decades of the nineteenth century, which did so much to sour relationships and create distrust between Germany and Britain, who regarded her traditional command of the seas as under challenge. Kaiser Wilhelm was at Kiel Week on his yacht when he heard the news of the assassination of Archduke Franz Ferdinand in June 1914, which proved the spark that ignited World War I. And four years later, in late October 1918, it was the actions of the sailors of the Baltic Fleet in Kiel that provided the spark for the revolution that toppled Wilhelm from his throne. Ordered to put to sea for a last-ditch naval battle, they mutinied and refused.

We enjoyed our time in Kiel, which is a bustling, busy city. From the windows of our hotel room we had a wonderful view of the Kiel Fjord with the comings and goings of cruise ships, ferries, and other shipping. Farther up the fjord towards the sea, in the Düsternbrook

14. The old schloss at Kiel was destroyed by bombs in 1944; the present building dates from the 1960s and is a concert hall.

area of the city is Kiel Schloss, which was once a residence of the dukes of Holstein. But like most of the buildings in central Kiel, the current schloss dates from after World War II. The old schloss, which dated back to the thirteenth century, was destroyed by fire after a bombing raid on 1 April 1944. During our tour we would come across several schlösser that suffered a similar fate in World War II, including others that have since been rebuilt.

The result at Kiel is an ugly, oblong, flat-roofed building of no apparent architectural merit, dating from the 1960s, which is used as a cultural centre and concert hall. The old schloss is visible only in the great stone blocks that were salvaged and used for the foundations of the 1960s brick building. So the schloss we see at Kiel today bears no resemblance to the building in old photographs from the turn of the twentieth century, when it was the home of Prince Henry (Heinrich) of Prussia. Henry was one of two Prussian princes called Heinrich whom we would come across on our tour. Each was the younger brother of a king of Prussia, and each lived in his older brother's shadow. To distinguish between them, I shall call the one who lived at Kiel Henry; and the other, who lived at Rheinsberg (see chapter 5), Heinrich.

Prince Henry was born in 1862 and was the third child and second son of Crown Prince and Princess Friedrich of Prussia. I have always felt rather sorry for Henry, as he was often 'pig in the middle' between the two strong characters in his family: his mother the crown princess (Queen Victoria's eldest daughter Vicky), and his elder brother Wilhelm (later Kaiser Wilhelm II). The two were often at loggerheads, and both expected Henry to be on their side. He seems to have dealt with this difficult situation by being easygoing and suggestible and by trying to keep in with both sides of the family. In December 1887 the crown princess wrote to her mother, Queen Victoria, that

Henry is quite nice and amiable now,....He is always nice when he has been with us some time, but not when he has been set up by others, and his head stuffed full of rubbish at Berlin....[46]

Henry married Princess Irene of Hesse-Darmstadt in the chapel at Schloss Charlottenburg on 24 May 1888. This is the year sometimes referred to as the Year of the Three Kaisers, since three German kaisers succeeded each other within a few months. Kaiser Wilhelm I (Henry's grandfather) died in March and was succeeded by his son, Friedrich III (Henry's father), who died just ninety-nine days later in June, to be succeeded by his son (Henry's elder brother) as Wilhelm II. Henry and Irene were married only three weeks before Kaiser Friedrich's death, and all the accounts of their wedding are dominated by his image. Despite being mortally ill and unable to breathe without the cannula in his throat, Kaiser Friedrich attended, dressed in full uniform, and stood during the ceremony. After the kaiser walked from the chapel, Prussian Field Marshall Moltke commented that he had

> seen many brave men, but none as brave as the Emperor has shown himself today.[47]

After their wedding, the newlyweds moved into Kiel schloss. Henry was a serving naval officer, so the location suited them well. The schloss would be their home for thirty years until they were forced out by revolution in November 1918.

Henry and Irene are a good illustration of the extraordinary inter-connectedness of Europe's royal families before World War I and the practice of what has been called 'marrying in and in' (marrying within a small and select royal circle and often within the same family).[48] The couple were first cousins (both their mothers were daughters of Queen Victoria), and they were closely related to the kings or queens of many European countries. Chart 6 shows these close family relationships in 1914 on the eve of World War I. Henry's brother was the German kaiser, and one of Irene's sisters was the tsarina of Russia. The king of Great Britain was a first cousin of both, and other cousins occupied the thrones of Greece, Norway, Romania, Spain, and Sweden. In hindsight it was a fragile house of cards, and the war would bring the whole edifice tumbling down, with families split on opposite sides. Some of these relatives would lose their thrones and even their lives.

PRINCE HENRY OF PRUSSIA AND PRINCESS IRENE OF HESSE.
GRANDCHILDREN OF QUEEN VICTORIA, BRIDE AND BRIDEGROOM.

15. Prince Henry of Prussia and his wife Irene pictured
at the time of their marriage.

It must have been very painful to Henry and Irene to be at war with Britain, where they were regular visitors and were well liked by their English relatives. Irene's mother, who was British, had died when she was still a child (twelve), and her grandmother, Queen Victoria, had then taken a close hand in her upbringing. Irene was a great support to her grandmother in her final months.[49] Henry got on well with his uncle, Edward VII (unlike his elder brother, Kaiser Wilhelm), and also with his cousin George V, with whom he had a lot in common. Of a similar age, they had known each other from childhood and both enjoyed naval careers. George had joined the British navy in 1877 when he was twelve, and Henry the German navy in 1876 when he was fourteen.

Henry was on a long summer holiday in England when Archduke Franz Ferdinand was assassinated and the international situation deteriorated. On his way back to Germany, he called in at Buckingham

Palace to discuss the situation with his cousin. The message he relayed back to the kaiser from this conversation with George V has been the subject of great controversy. Henry incorrectly reported the king as having said that Britain would try to keep out of the coming conflict and stay neutral. This was only wishful thinking on Henry's part and more what he (and his brother, the kaiser) wanted to hear than what George had actually said. War was declared on 4 August with Britain, France, and Russia on one side against Germany and Austria.

All of Irene's three sisters were on the opposite side to Germany in the conflict. Her eldest sister, Victoria, was married to Prince Louis of Battenberg, who was the First Sea Lord of the British Admiralty (head of the British navy). Although a German prince by birth, Louis had joined the British navy and by 1914 he had served for forty-six years. But after war was declared, Louis's German birth and close family relationship with Henry, who had been appointed naval Commander-in-Chief of the German Baltic fleet, caused an outcry in Britain and he was forced to resign. This was portrayed as unfair and a tragedy for Louis, but with a modern eye I cannot be too sympathetic. There was clearly a conflict of interest, and I do wonder what secrets had passed when the two men chatted over the family dinner table for years!

Irene's other two sisters were both in Russia. Her elder sister, Ella, had married Grand Duke Serge, who was an uncle of Tsar Nicholas II. After Serge was assassinated by terrorists in 1905, Ella became a nun and founded a convent in Moscow. Irene's younger sister, Alix, had married the tsar himself to become Tsarina Alexandra Feodorovna. As the war went on Alix's German roots contributed to her increasing unpopularity in her adopted country. Reviled as *the German woman*, she was suspected of treason and blamed for everything that went wrong.[50] After the March 1917 revolution the new provisional Russian government hoped to send Alix, her husband, and their five children into exile in Britain, but King George V was not in favour. With revolution in the air, he was nervous about his own throne and fast distancing himself from his German connections.

The Schleswig-Holstein Ducal Families

The Schleswig-Holstein ducal families were part of the royal house of Oldenburg. This was divided into numerous branches (see chart 3), and those associated with Schleswig-Holstein took their names from their ancestral schlösser. So the (Schleswig) Holstein-Gottorf branch (both the senior line who became tsars of Russia, and the junior line who became dukes of Oldenburg) took their name from Schloss Gottorf in Holstein, which is now a wonderful museum and well worth a visit. The Schleswig-Holstein-Sonderburg-Augustenburg line took theirs from the two schlösser of those names that nowadays fall just on the Danish side of the border with Schleswig. And the Schleswig-Holstein-Glücksburg branch took their name from Schloss Glücksburg, which is just on the German side of the same border. To make things simpler, I shall shorten the last two of these hyphenated names to Augustenburg and Glücksburg.

Both the Augustenburg and the Glücksburg families were involved in the Schleswig-Holstein question (see appendix D). The Augustenburgs hoped to become dukes of an independent Schleswig-Holstein, and the Glücksburgs did become kings of Denmark after the male line of the previous royal family died out. The duke of Augustenburg also had a claim to the Danish throne, but he fought against Denmark in the First War of Schleswig-Holstein, which naturally made him unpopular with the Danes. So his claim to their throne was overlooked in favour of a prince from the Glücksburg family. Under the London Protocol of 1852, endorsed by the Great Powers at the end of the first war, Prince Christian of Glücksburg was designated successor to the childless King Frederick VII of Denmark, and it was agreed that the two duchies of Schleswig-Holstein would stay with Denmark. The duke of Augustenburg renounced his claims to these.

However this still did not settle the issue, and the Second War of Schleswig-Holstein erupted only a few years later. Duke Friedrich VIII of Augustenburg then unsuccessfully revived the claim to be duke of Schleswig-Holstein which his father had renounced. After Denmark's defeat in the Second War, the duchies were annexed and became part of Prussia.

That same year George V changed the surname of the British royal family from Saxe-Coburg-Gotha to the much more English-sounding Windsor. The Russians were abandoned to their fate and in July 1918, Alix with all her family and some loyal servants, and Ella with other members of the Romanov family, were murdered by the Bolsheviks.

When revolution broke out in Germany at the end of the war, Henry and Irene and their family were at Kiel. They fled by car to take refuge a few miles north at their private summer home at Hemmelmark. Their car is said to have been fired at on the way.[51] Henry had purchased an estate there in 1896 and a few years later built a large house in what was called the English style. He gave a formal undertaking to the new German government not to interfere in politics, and the couple lived quietly at Hemmelmark for the rest of their lives. Both are buried in the family mausoleum that Henry built in the grounds, together with the youngest of their three sons. Little Henry suffered from haemophilia and died aged four in 1904 after an accident playing with his two elder brothers at Schloss Kiel. Like her sister Alix, the tsarina of Russia, Irene was a carrier of this dreadful disease. We found the hamlet of Hemmelmark, but the schloss (which is privately owned and not open to the public) is not visible from the road.

Wasserschloss Glücksburg

The wasserschloss (or water castle) at Glücksburg truly deserves its name; the granite foundations rise directly out of the lake on three sides. Only on the fourth side is the schloss connected by a narrow causeway to the shore. With its tall white walls reflected in the water, Glücksburg looks rather like a castle in a fairy tale; it is an idyllic setting.

Glücksburg is situated on the Flensburg Fjord, on the eastern (Baltic) shore of the Jutland Peninsula. It is just south of the present-day border with Denmark, and over the centuries its history has been inextricably bound up with that country. The schloss was built in the

1580s by Duke Johann (or Hans) the Younger of Oldenburg, who was a younger son of the Danish king Christian III. The initials of the duke's motto are carved in stone above the entrance—GGGMF, which stands for *Gott Gebe Glück Mit Frieden*, or *God Grant Happiness and Peace*. So the name of the schloss means Happiness Castle.

The schloss was the residence of the descendants of Johann the Younger until this elder Glücksburg line died out and it reverted to the Danish crown. In 1825 the Danish king Frederik VI recreated the title and gave the schloss to Duke Wilhelm of Schleswig-Holstein-Sonderburg-Beck, who became the first duke and founder of the younger Glücksburg line. Frederik VI thought highly of Wilhelm, who was also his brother-in-law as well as a distant relative.[52] Frederik VI was married to Marie of Hesse-Kassel, and Wilhelm to her younger sister Luise.

16. The wasserschloss (or water castle) at Glücksburg truly deserves its name; the foundations rise directly out of the lake on three sides.

The new duke of Glücksburg and his wife had a large family and were poor by royal standards. Wilhelm was an army officer with no expectation of any inheritance, and before their move to Schloss Glücksburg the couple had lived with her parents. There are several stories about how the family were forced to make economies. For example, the boys could not all attend the same dance because the required formal wear meant white gloves, and there were not enough pairs to go round. On Wilhelm's early death from pneumonia in 1831, aged only forty-six, Duchess Luise was left with ten children aged between two and twenty. She reduced the staff at Glücksburg to just three servants and huddled her family into the few rooms she could afford to heat. She must have seen it as a boon when her sister and brother-in-law, King Frederik VI and Queen Marie, offered to bring one of her sons to Denmark and take charge of his education.

The story of how Prince Christian of Glücksburg became one of Europe's most respected monarchs is one of royal history's great sur-

17. A romantic view of Glücksburg in an old picture, with swans on the lake.

prises. Christian was the fourth son of Wilhelm and Luise, and when he was born in 1818 there didn't seem the remotest chance that he would one day become king of Denmark. It was true that his uncle, Frederik VI, had no surviving sons, but there were male heirs much closer to the throne and, of course, even should the succession come down to Christian's branch of the family (which was unlikely), he had three older brothers. But Christian's life changed after his father died and, at thirteen years old, he moved to Copenhagen under his uncle's protection.

56

The sponsorship of Frederik VI, which was continued after his death by the next king, Christian VIII, brought Christian to the notice of the international royal community, where his good looks, charm, and modest ways gained him good marks.[53] In 1838 he represented Denmark at Queen Victoria's coronation, and in 1842 he went to St Petersburg for Tsar Nicholas I's silver wedding celebrations. It seemed that the two kings (Frederik VI and Christian VIII) wanted to push forward the honest and upright Christian of Glücksburg at the expense of the dissolute and scandal-ridden Frederik (later Frederik VII), who was the son of Christian VIII and the next heir.[54]

In 1842 Christian married Princess Luise of Hesse-Kassel, who (like himself) was a descendant of King Frederik V of Denmark in the female line (see chart 7). It would prove a truly happy marriage and the couple were devoted to each other. But it was also a smart move that assisted Christian's candidacy for the throne. Danish royal law provided that if the male line died out, then the succession would pass to the closest entitled male of the female line. This was Luise's brother, but in 1851 he renounced his claim in favour of his sister and her husband. In 1852, at the end of the First Schleswig-Holstein War, Christian was named as heir to the Danish throne and became known as the Prince of Denmark. He succeeded as Christian IX when King Frederik VII, who was the last male in the branch of the Oldenburg family that had provided kings of Denmark since 1460, died without an heir in 1863. A new branch of the house took over, and another minor German duke succeeded to a European throne!

To help the reader understand Christian's path to the throne, I have provided a family tree (chart 7) that shows the Danish kings from Frederik V up to Christian IX, in their date order and how they were related. Their reign numbers are as important as their names since from 1460 until 1972 (when the present Queen Margrethe II came to the throne), all the monarchs of Denmark were called either Christian or Frederik.

The years before and after his succession were not easy ones for Christian IX. Tensions ran high between Denmark and Germany over

Schleswig-Holstein, and, having been born on one side and adopted into the other, Christian was viewed ambivalently by both sides. In the duchies he was known derisively as the Protocol Prince.[55] His Glücksburg brothers fought against Denmark on the side of the duchies in the first war of 1848–1851, and quite understandably, they were persona non grata in Denmark afterwards. Schloss Glücksburg suffered considerable damage during the conflict and the family had to leave. It was then taken over by the king of Denmark, Frederik VII, who refurbished it and used it as a summer home, and he died there in 1863. In the second Schleswig-Holstein War the schloss was used as a military hospital and barracks by the Prussians and Austrians, and it was not until 1871 that it was returned and the Glücksburgs moved back in.[56]

When Christian came to the throne the second war was imminent, and it did not help his popularity in Denmark that he was born a German prince. Denmark suffered a disastrous defeat at the hands of Prussia and Austria, losing around 40 per cent of her territory and population. Anti-monarchy demonstrations were held in Copenhagen, the king's children were insulted and spat at in the streets, and the family had to have police protection. Christian never forgot the traumatic events of 1864 and campaigned for the rest of his life for the return of the duchies. But he survived this early crisis in his reign and was king of Denmark for forty-three years, until his death in 1906.

The success of Christian's children earned him the sobriquet of Father-in-law of Europe and increased his standing at home and abroad. They were a great success in the European royalty stakes and of his six children, two became kings and two became queens consort. His eldest son succeeded him as Frederik VIII, his middle son was elected King George I of Greece (in place of the deposed King Otto), and only the youngest (Valdemar) refused a throne, turning down the crowns of Bulgaria and Norway. Christian's three daughters married well. The eldest was the beautiful Alexandra (known as Alix), who became queen of Great Britain (see Schloss Reinhardsbrunn). The middle daughter (Dagmar, known as Minnie) became Tsarina Marie Feodorovna of

18. Alexandra, the beautiful eldest daughter of Prince Christian of Glücksburg, married the Prince of Wales in the same year that her father became the king of Denmark and her brother the king of Greece.

Russia, and only the youngest (Thyra) did not marry a king but the ex-crown prince of Hannover. When Alix married Queen Victoria's eldest son, Bertie (the prince of Wales), in 1863, Victoria was worried that a Danish princess in the family might cause trouble; she had wanted Bertie to follow the longstanding practice for the British royal family and marry a German princess. And she was right to be concerned. With her eldest daughter, Vicky, married to the crown prince of Prussia, and Bertie to the Danish king's daughter, her children's loyalties were split over the conflict in Schleswig-Holstein. And it got even more complicated and divisive when in 1865 another daughter (Helena) became engaged to the brother of the third player in the drama of the duchies, the duke of Augustenburg. No wonder Victoria bemoaned that Alix was not German for the sake of 'peace and harmony in the family!'[57]

In 1885 Christian's nephew Friedrich Ferdinand, the fourth duke of Glücksburg in the new line, married Caroline Mathilde (known in the family as Calma) of Augustenburg. Her sister Dona (Empress Auguste Viktoria of Germany) then became a regular visitor to Glücksburg, and even today one of the rooms on the first floor and the adjoining tower are called the Empress's Salon and the Empress's Tower, after her. Dona's husband, Kaiser Wilhelm II, was constantly on the move travelling from place to place, and he rarely took her with him. The schloss is of an unusual construction and when cut through, it looks like three oblongs, long sides together, with a small octagonal tower in each corner. As a result the floor plan consists of a long central room with smaller square rooms to either side, plus the four tower rooms. The interiors at Glücksburg are cosy and charming, with low vaulted ceilings, and I found it easy to imagine the two sisters (Dona and Calma) sitting there chatting and sewing while their children played around their feet.

I had long wanted to visit Glücksburg, but it was a mixed experience. This was the first schloss on our tour that was very busy with visitors, and there was also a wedding party, with a radiant bride in her wedding dress and an ambulance as the unusual going-away vehicle. It all felt a bit disorganised and chaotic. Most of the visitors were doing guided tours in German, but instead we were given very rushed instructions by a smartly uniformed gentleman on the door. 'You go first here, then there, then there, then upstairs....' Of course we could not take it all in so fast, and as a result I think we may have missed some rooms.

The policy of no photographs inside the schloss was also a disappointment. All visitors like to take photos as a reminder of their holiday, and I have an extra reason as it saves me from taking lots of notes; when I get home I use the photos to jog my memory. Another bugbear was the awful felt overshoes that visitors had to wear to protect the wooden floors. I heartily dislike these because I am always afraid I will slip and fall over. I understand the need to protect the floors, but there must be a better and less dangerous way to do this—perhaps a strip of carpet for visitors to walk on. It beats me how these old-fashioned slippers can possibly pass a modern health-and-safety inspection.

How German Dukes Took Over Many European Thrones

The story of how Christian of Glücksburg became king of Denmark was the fourth time on our tour that we had come across a German duke who became the king of another European country. The others are Otto of Bavaria (Greece), Karl Peter Ulrich (Russia), and Adolf Friedrich (Sweden) of Holstein-Gottorf.

Hereditary monarchy was considered to be the natural and the best form of government. So when a royal line died out, or a new country became independent, the search would be on to find a king. This might be by tracing descent through the female line, as when the elector of Hannover became George I of Great Britain in 1714 (see Schloss I). His mother was the daughter of the daughter of James I and the nearest eligible Protestant claimant.

When a new country became independent, such as Greece in the 1830s, then the choice was more likely to be made by diplomacy, as the candidate had to be acceptable to the Great Powers. After King Otto was deposed in 1862 his throne was offered to Queen Victoria's second son, in the hope that the connection with Great Britain would prove advantageous to Greece. When this was refused, it was offered to another German duke, Vilhelm of Glücksburg, who became King George I.

There are many other examples, such as Leopold of Saxe-Coburg, who became king of Belgium in 1831, and Karl of Hohenzollern-Sigmaringen, who became the ruling prince of Romania in 1866. The practice persisted right up until the end of the old order. When the Finns became independent from Russia during World War I, they elected Friedrich Karl of Hesse-Kassel as king of Finland. With Germany's defeat, he had to renounce the throne before he ever got to his new country. Finland became a republic.

Schloss vor Husum

19. Schloss vor Husum is built of brick in the Dutch Renaissance style, with interspersed horizontal courses of cream-coloured sandstone

On our way down the Jutland Peninsula from Glücksburg to Kiel, we stopped at Husum on the west coast of Schleswig, where we visited the Schloss vor Husum. Its name means the Castle outside Husum, because that's where it was when originally built. Husum dates from the 1580s and is built of brick with interspersed horizontal courses of cream-coloured sandstone, in what is called the Dutch Renaissance style. The schloss is long and low, with short protruding wings at both ends and a single tower in the centre that rises several stories above it. Over the main door is a beautiful brick arch with an intricately carved stone coat of arms.

The town of Husum was the birthplace of Theodor Storm (1817–1888), who was one of the most important German writers of the nine-teenth century. Storm lived there for many years and used it as the setting for some of his stories and poems. There is a charming small knot garden to one side of the schloss with a symmetrical pattern of beds, paths, lawn, and hedging. An interesting feature is the stones inset into a central path, each engraved with a short saying in German about castles or gardens. They include a verse from Storm's famous poem called 'The Nightingale'. Here is the verse, both in the original German and then as my husband translated it.

Das macht, es hat die Nachtigall	It is because the nightingale
Die ganze Nacht gesungen.	Sang all night long.
Da sind von ihren süssen Schall	From her sweet song
Da sind in Hall und Widerhall	Echoing and re-echoing
Die Rosen aufgesprungen.	The roses burst into bloom.

Schloss vor Husum was built by Adolf I, who was the first duke of Schleswig-Holstein-Gottorf (for short, Holstein-Gottorf). As the reader will have gathered, the house of Oldenburg has a complex history, with new branches forming and old branches dying out across the centuries. The Holstein-Gottorf branch came into existence in 1544 when—after the king of Denmark's death—a new duchy of that name was created for his younger son, who became Duke Adolf I. After Adolf's death the Holstein-Gottorf branch itself split into two, creating a senior line who remained dukes of Holstein-Gottorf, and a junior line who became prince-bishops of Lübeck.

I was fortunate to find a leaflet that has been a huge help in

20. The main door with brick arch and coat of arms.

understanding how all these pieces fit together.[58] Although in German, the information is presented in a visual way which makes it easy to follow, and I used this helpful leaflet as a source for chart 3.

Husum was used as an occasional residence by the dukes of Holstein-Gottorf and later as a dower house for their widows. Duchess

Augusta lived there for more than twenty years in the first half of the seventeenth century (1616–1639). She was the widow of Johann Adolf (the son of Adolf I) and a Danish princess connected by birth to many of Europe's royal families. She created a sophisticated and cultured court at Husum and is responsible for the elaborate carved stone and alabaster fireplaces, which are such an attractive feature of the schloss today.

Husum passed to the Danish crown in 1721 after the Great Northern War, when the dukes of Holstein-Gottorf lost part of their territory in Schleswig to Denmark. By the middle of the century the schloss was

21. The elaborate carved stone fireplaces at Husum were saved on the orders of the king of Denmark.

in a very poor state of repair when it was saved and restored by King Frederik V of Denmark. He apparently did this against the advice of his ministers, who recommended demolition as a cheaper option.

It is not known why Frederik wanted to use the schloss as a royal residence, but one idea is because of its location on the coast of the North Sea. Frederik's first wife, Queen Louise, was a British princess (the daughter of George II), and Husum would have been a convenient place to embark by boat on a trip to her home country.[59]

So the schloss was given a major overhaul and, fortunately for us, Frederik resisted the suggestion from his architect to remove the stone fireplaces.[60] At the same time, a formal suite of rooms known as the *Staatsappartement* (or state apartments) was created, which the king could use to hold his court on formal occasions. These rooms are still part of the visitors' tour today.

The schloss at Husum is a relaxed and friendly place. We received a very warm welcome and the lady in the ticket office went to some trouble to search out a handout in English for us to use.[61] This included both a brief history of the schloss and also a suggested tour route. With the help of the handout, we wandered happily around at our own pace. We also enjoyed a personal tour from the very enthusiastic and knowledgeable curator of a most unusual small museum that is housed in the schloss.

This one-room museum, which is situated next to the ticket office and shop, is called Pole Poppenspäler (or Paul the Puppeteer) after one of Theodor Storm's most famous stories, set in a marionette theatre. The museum houses a fascinating collection of glove puppets and marionettes from different countries around the world, some hundreds of years old and some very modern. The curator demonstrated several of them for us. The difference between the two is that a puppet is operated by the hand of the puppeteer, which goes inside it like a glove, while a marionette is controlled by strings attached to its limbs. The museum is a year-round legacy of the annual international festival of puppets and marionettes which is held in Husum every September and has been going for more than thirty years (since 1983). Every day for the duration of the festival there are numerous shows at different locations around the town, including the schloss.

Storm was very fond of his hometown and wrote that his heart would always remain in Husum, with its happy memories of his youth. We liked it there too.

The Blome Schlösser: Finding a Use in the Twenty-First Century

While we were exploring the countryside around Kiel in Holstein, we came across two beautiful schlösser called Blomenburg and Salzau. Both once belonged to the grafs von Blome (one of the oldest Holstein noble families), and both were currently empty and looking for a commercial use to support their upkeep. With so many schlösser in Germany, this is a very real problem.

Blomenburg (see picture) is on the south side of Lake Selenter. It was built in the 1840s as a summer home for Graf Otto von Blome. There was a fashion then for building in a romanticised version of the past, and Blomenburg is a miniature English Tudor castle, complete with turrets, towers, and battlements. Until a few years ago, it was used as a technology centre, but the venture failed and a new commercial use for the schloss was being sought.

By chance we bumped into the current owner during our visit, and he very kindly let us look inside. The schloss has been beautifully restored, retaining the original but also adding modern, and often quirky, features. Next door to the original building is the modern office block of the technology centre, which is linked to the schloss by a wonderful glass bridge across the garden, called 'the bridge of light'. When we came outside, my husband commented that Blomenburg would be a good location for a James Bond movie.

On the other side of the lake is Schloss Salzau, which was also built by Graf Otto in the 1880s after the previous building on the site burned down.

Salzau is owned by the state government of Schleswig-Holstein and was for many years a thriving cultural centre, providing a popular venue for music festivals and jazz concerts. But the costs of maintenance were high and eventually the state claimed that these were unaffordable, so the centre was closed and the schloss put up for sale.

4

MECKLENBURG-
WESTERN POMERANIA AND
THE HOUSE OF
MECKLENBURG-STRELITZ

From Kiel on the Jutland peninsula we drove east along the coast towards our next destination. Just after Lübeck we crossed the state boundary into Mecklenburg-Western Pomerania (Mecklenburg-Vorpommern in German), and for the first time on this trip we were in a part of Germany which, before reunification in 1990, was behind the Iron Curtain. The watchtowers and the border guards have gone, but the old boundary is still commemorated by signs saying Inner Deutscher Grenze, or Intra-German Border. We drove across where, at its northern point, the old border met the Baltic Sea.

My husband and I knew little about Mecklenburg-Western Pomerania before we went on our schloss tours. It is one of the most beautiful parts of Germany, with a long coastline along the Baltic Sea fringed with beaches of white sand and dotted with islands. On our first tour we stayed in the seaside resort of Heiligendamm (see *Schloss I*), which straightaway became one of our favourite places. On this trip, however, we were headed for what is often called the Land of a Thousand Lakes, or the Mecklenburg Lake District.

This is the largest lake area in central Europe, and it has always been sparsely populated and underdeveloped. Chancellor Bismarck of Prussia is supposed to have once said that it was so remote and backward that the world would probably end there one hundred years later than everywhere else.[62] Today this wonderful natural environment of lakes, marshes, and forests, with its abundance of wildlife, is a protected natural park.

The Mecklenburg Lake District was once the independent duchy of Mecklenburg-Strelitz, with its own royal family. Although only a small and landlocked state surrounded by larger and more powerful neighbours, Mecklenburg-Strelitz was well connected with the great powers of Europe through family relationships. While there, we would visit schlösser associated with three princesses from this small principality—one was born there, one died there, and one lived there for three-quarters of a century. Please see chart 8 for a simplified genealogy of these three princesses.

Schlossinsel Mirow

The first of the princesses was Sophie Charlotte of Mecklenburg-Strelitz, and she was born in Mirow on 19 May 1744. As the younger daughter of a younger brother of the duke of a small principality, she was not a very important princess, but she would come to occupy one of the greatest positions in the eighteenth-century world. For Sophie Charlotte was picked from a list to marry the king of England.

The schloss was built for her grandmother, Duchess Christiane Emilie, after she was widowed in 1708. Christiane was the third wife of the first duke of Mecklenburg-Strelitz (Adolphus Friedrich II) and was much younger than her husband. After his death she moved to Mirow with her baby son, Karl, who became known as the Prince of Mirow. As a younger son Karl had limited prospects, but over time these started to look better as it became clear that he would be the heir to his older half-brother, Adolphus Friedrich III, who had no sons to succeed him. In fact Karl died just a few months before his half-brother in 1752, so it was Karl's eldest son who became the new duke, Adolphus Friedrich IV. But it was Karl's eighth child, Sophie Charlotte, who would really transform the family fortunes.

22. Mirow in the Mecklenburg Lake District was built for the widow of the first duke of Mecklenburg-Strelitz.

When King George III succeeded to the British throne in October 1760, Sophie Charlotte was sixteen years old. The twenty-two-year-old king was in a hurry to get married. He had recently fallen desperately in love with a fourteen-year-old earl's daughter, Lady Sarah Lennox, but had been told that marriage to her was impossible. No one could expect the king to remain chaste forever, and, to guard against any future misalliances, it was important that he be found a suitable wife. So the eligible European princesses were reviewed to identify possible candidates. Sophie Charlotte was not initially thought of for the role but her family had links with Hannover (George's second kingdom), and at a late stage her name was put forward by the minister for Hannover.

The process by which the new queen was selected is fascinating and sounds like a modern-day business proposal. A short list of eligible princesses was drawn up and information gathered to assess each of them against the key requirements. The new queen had to be of the right age and religion, have an impeccable pedigree, and look likely to be a good breeder. The king also said he wanted a wife 'with a good understanding, a pleasant disposition and no idea of meddling in public affairs.'[63]

As the preferred candidates were reviewed and crossed off for one reason or another, Sophie Charlotte's name came up the list. One princess was eliminated because her grandfather had married a commoner, another for fear of mental instability in her family, and a third after her character was described as 'obstinate and disobliging'.[64] Sophie Charlotte came from a small and unimportant state, and little was known about her, which probably worked to her advantage. When good reports of her arrived in response to enquiries, George III made up his mind quickly and announced their betrothal.

Events moved at a dizzying speed for the inexperienced princess from a tiny court. The emissary from George III arrived in Mecklenburg-Strelitz in June 1761 to make the necessary enquiries about her. Just two months later, she left her old home as a bride-to-be to travel to England. Nothing was allowed to stand in the way of an early wedding, not even the death of her mother on 29 June. It has been said that the young and inexperienced Lady Diana Spencer was put under too much pressure when she married Prince Charles in 1981, and she had to cope with becoming princess of Wales and the mother of a future king of Great Britain within a year. Sophie Charlotte of Mecklenburg-

Strelitz went through a baptism of fire. She was married on the same day that she met her future husband for the first time; was crowned queen alongside him two weeks later; and gave birth to a prince of Wales eleven months after that!

23. Princess Sophie Charlotte of Mecklenburg-Strelitz was picked from a list to marry the king of England.

On 16 August 1761 Sophie Charlotte set out from her old home, accompanied by the English ambassador who had been sent to escort her. They travelled by carriage to the North Sea coast of Hannover, where British ships were waiting. The sea crossing was appalling, and only after two weeks of gales and storms did she land in England at Harwich on 7 September. She spoke no English and must have been exhausted, but as the new queen she was immediately the centre of attention.

In the afternoon of the following day, 8 September, the princess arrived at St James's Palace in London, where she met her fiancé for the first time and was introduced to his family. At about nine that same evening she walked through the palace, in the centre of a grand procession, to be married in the Chapel Royal. In front of her were drums and trumpets, maids of honour, peeresses, and the lord chamberlain; behind her were ten unmarried daughters of dukes and earls.[65] Up until now, her demeanour had impressed everyone who saw her; she was described as dignified, kind, and sincere, and with an even temper. But as she walked to her wedding, on the arm of the duke of York and dressed in her wedding finery, she momentarily faltered. Perhaps at that moment everything overwhelmed her. The duke tried to steady her by repeating the words, 'Courage, Princess' over and over again.[66]

It is clear from the reports that were sent to England that Sophie Charlotte was not considered to be a beauty by the standards of the day. She was described as amiable and agreeable to look at, but the implication is that she was plain. An early biography published in 1819, only a year after her death, describes her features:

'...the nose a little flat, and turned up at the point; the mouth rather large, with rosy lips, and very fine teeth.[67]

She also had lovely hair, a tress of which was sent to George III before their marriage. When writing her biography of Queen Charlotte, published in 1975, Olwen Hedley found the tress preserved in a box in the royal collection. Based on the queen's appearance in some portraits, it has been suggested more recently that she may have had some African ancestry. The suggestion is that one of her fifteenth-century ancestors may have been a Moor from North Africa. Even if it is the case, it is so many generations removed that it would not be a major part of her genetic makeup.[68]

The marriage was a meteoric stroke of luck for the house of Mecklenburg-Strelitz even though Sophie Charlotte's brother, Duke Adolphus Friedrich IV, had to put himself in debt to fund her dowry. He was made a Knight of the Garter, and her next brother, Karl, became governor of Hannover. The only casualty seems to have been Sophie Charlotte's elder sister, Christiane. At twenty-five, she had been too old to be considered for George III, but she had already formed an attachment to a Scottish peer. After her sister's engagement, this was brought to an end. It was unthinkable that the sister-in-law of a British king could be married to his subject![69] Poor Christiane never married; perhaps no wonder that in her letters Queen Charlotte later described her sister as nagging, sickly, and interfering.[70]

The Royal House of Mecklenburg-Strelitz

The principality of Mecklenburg-Strelitz was created in 1701 to settle a lengthy dispute over inheritance in the house of Mecklenburg. The small new state was awarded to Duke Adolphus Friedrich II, who was the uncle of the reigning duke of Mecklenburg. The reigning duke retained the larger, western part of the family lands, called Mecklenburg-Schwerin, with the capital in Schwerin. The eastern and smaller part went to his uncle. The new Duke Adolf Friedrich II decided to have his capital in the little town of Strelitz, and the new duchy was called Mecklenburg-Strelitz. This was the last division of lands in the house and from now on, each of the two Mecklenburg lines would descend by primogeniture (inheritance by the firstborn male heir). Both would survive until the end of the German monarchy in 1918. My first book (Schloss I) includes schlösser in Mecklenburg-Schwerin. In this second book (Schloss II), we visit schlösser in Mecklenburg-Strelitz.

It is confusing that the first duke of Mecklenburg-Strelitz was called the second (Adolphus Friedrich II), but this was probably to distinguish him from his father, who was also Adolphus Friedrich. It was the most popular name in this branch of the family. There would be eight reigning dukes of Mecklenburg-Strelitz in all, and five were called Adolphus Friedrich. The remaining three were Karl, Georg, and Friedrich Wilhelm. The fourth duke, who was Karl, was promoted to grand duke in 1815, at the end of the Napoleonic Wars.

Please see chart 9 for the eight dukes of Mecklenburg-Strelitz.

King George III and Queen Charlotte became a devoted and faithful couple. He never took a mistress, and she fulfilled her dynastic responsibilities by giving birth to fifteen children. But George suffered from bouts of illness, and in later years this overshadowed their lives and they became estranged. The general view now is that he had porphyria, a rare metabolic disorder that produces both physical and mental symptoms. The disease was not identified until well into the twentieth century and in George's case was diagnosed as madness. The queen was frightened by his symptoms when he was in the throes of the illness, and when he recovered, he partially blamed her for allowing the cruel treatments for mental illness to which he was subjected. Queen Charlotte became a lonely and unhappy old woman who behaved badly to her grown-up children and prevented her daughters from marrying.

There are many portraits of Queen Charlotte, but the one I find most compelling is in the National Gallery and was painted by Sir Thomas Lawrence in 1789. The queen looks older than her forty-five years, rather haggard, and even dishevelled. Her husband had only recently recovered from the first major bout of his illness, and it is the face of a woman who has been through a traumatic experience. The king and queen never liked this picture and, unusually, did not buy it from the artist when it was finished. But fortunately it has ended up in the national collection.

It has always surprised me that Queen Charlotte is not a better-known queen of England, despite being queen consort for fifty-seven years. There seem to be far fewer books written about her, for example, than about her disreputable daughter-in-law Caroline of Brunswick, who was queen consort for only eighteen months. We came across Caroline later in our tour (see chapter 7). Charlotte had many notable achievements for which she ought to be remembered. Having survived fifteen pregnancies in twenty-one years, she became patron of a small lying-in hospital, saving it from financial difficulties and securing its future. It went on to become the renowned Queen Charlotte's Maternity Hospital in West London, where my own daughter was born.

The queen was also a keen botanist who played an important part in building up a botanical collection in one of the royal palaces that later became the world-famous Kew Gardens. She was sometimes called the Queen of Botany. Travellers brought back exotic plants from all parts of the world to Kew. When the beautiful bird of paradise flower was introduced to the collection from South Africa in the 1770s, it was named Strelitza reginae by the director, Joseph Banks, in her honour. Charlotte later sent the plant as a gift to her home in Mecklenburg-Strelitz.[71]

The schloss at Mirow is in a picturesque setting, on a small island close to the shore of the Mirower See. It is called Schlossinsel Mirow because *schlossinsel* means island castle. Entry is across a short bridge and then through an arched gatehouse. Once inside we climbed some steps up a grassy mound to get our first view of the schloss. It lay before us, small, symmetrical, pristine, and cute, looking just like a dolls' house of a schloss. It felt almost as if, like a dolls' house, we could open up the front to reveal the rooms inside.

After the abolition of the German monarchy in 1918, the schlossinsel went into a long period of decline and neglect. No longer a palace it was put to other uses, including as a military hospital, an officers' mess, and an old people's home. But after the fall of the Iron Curtain and the reunification of Germany in 1990, its fortunes improved when it was acquired by the new federal state of Mecklenburg-Pomerania. After a renovation lasting many years it was due to open to the public as a museum the month after we were there, in June 2014. Everything looked ready—only the gardeners were putting the last-minute touches to the gardens. It was frustrating to be there so close to the opening, especially as this had happened to us before (see *Schloss I*, where we missed the opening of the new schloss in Herrenhausen by a similar margin).

The nearby Lower Palace, where Queen Charlotte was born, is a stark contrast to the main schlossinsel. Once proudly remodelled by the third duke as his family's ancestral home, this now looks sad and neglected. A plaque outside records it as Queen Charlotte's birthplace. Another sign said that the building was up for sale.

24. The Lower Palace where Queen Charlotte lived as a child
has not been restored and looked sad and neglected.

Although we were a month too early for the reopening of the schlossinsel, we were able to visit an exhibition in the cavalier house. This excellent exhibition is about the history of the duchy and the princesses of Mecklenburg-Strelitz who became queens of foreign countries, including Queen Charlotte. The exhibition was well set out, had interesting content, and made good use of interactive media. I pressed buttons and answered multiple-choice questions, and it was all good fun. Although there was no guidebook in English, all the material on all the displays was translated.

Hohenzieritz

Our second princess associated with Mecklenburg-Strelitz was Luise, and we went to Schloss Hohenzieritz to find out more about her story. Although Luise visited the schloss only once or twice in her life, it will always be connected with her because it is where she died, aged thirty-four, on 19 July 1810. She was Queen Luise, the best-loved and most famous queen of Prussia.

Hohenzieritz was a surprise gift to Luise's father, Karl, from his elder brother, Duke Adolphus Friedrich IV of Mecklenburg-Strelitz. Karl was Queen Charlotte's second brother, born in 1741, and her marriage changed his life. Up to that point he was just a landless younger son, with few expectations and destined for a military career. Aged twenty, he held a junior rank in the Hanoverian army. After the marriage he obtained the lucrative post of governor of Hannover, which carried a large salary, from his brother-in-law, George III. Helped by their close family connections to the throne of England, two of his daughters would marry kings.

Hohenzieritz was Karl's summer home for forty-six years. It was a modest estate when his brother gave it to him in 1770, but Karl transformed the manor house into a grand palace and replaced the small geometric baroque garden with a large English landscape park. We had already heard about the craze for this new style of gardening from our visit to Oldenburg (see chapter 2). Karl was among the very first to introduce it to Germany. He visited his sister Queen Charlotte in London in 1771, the year after he was given Hohenzieritz, and was inspired by her gardens at Richmond and Kew. So he brought back the idea to have an English landscape garden at Hohenzieritz and also an English landscape gardener to help create it. This was the Scottish botanist-gardener Archibald Thomson, who was a pupil of the most famous English landscape gardener of all, Lancelot (Capability) Brown.[72]

Karl became the fourth duke of Mecklenburg-Strelitz in 1794, after his elder brother Adolphus Friedrich IV died. He had by then known great sorrow, with the deaths of both his wives, who were sisters, as a result of pregnancy and childbirth. Karl went on a long sabbatical, stepping aside from his duties and travelling. He never looked for a third wife and he erected a touching monument to the two who had died, as well as to his five children who died young, in the garden at Hohenzieritz. This is called Hope Comforts Sorrow. Before many more years had passed there would be another monument in the garden, this time for his dead grown-up daughter, Luise.

25. Hohenzieritz was the summer home of Grand Duke Karl
of Mecklenburg-Strelitz.

Luise was born in Hannover on 10 March 1776, during the time
that her father was the governor there. Her mother was his first wife,
who died when Luise was six. Karl got married again quickly, to his
dead wife's sister, but after her death the family was split up. Luise was
brought up by her grandmother in Hesse and did not even visit her
home country of Mecklenburg-Strelitz until she was an adult. Aged
seventeen, Luise made a grand dynastic marriage to Crown Prince
Friedrich Wilhelm of Prussia, and the couple became king and queen
of Prussia in 1797.

Luise was unfortunate to live in a time when Europe was in chaos
following the French Revolution and Napoleon's armies were march-
ing across Germany. In 1806 the Prussian army suffered a crushing
defeat at the twin battles of Jena-Auerstadt, and Prussia was invaded.
Luise and her family were forced to flee as Napoleon advanced to occupy

their capital, Berlin. It was three years before they were able to return, following a humiliating peace treaty. Luise had swallowed her pride and met with Napoleon privately to intercede for her adopted country, but had achieved nothing. On 23 December 1809, sixteen years almost to the day after she had entered Berlin to be married, Friedrich Wilhelm and Luise re-entered their capital to the cheers of Berliners. It was a sad homecoming. She wrote that they were still miserable but at least they were miserable in better surroundings.[73] Exactly a year later, on 23 December 1810, her body would be interred in the newly built mausoleum at Schloss Charlottenburg in Berlin (see *Schloss I*).

In the summer of 1810, Luise was excited about a holiday with her father in Mecklenburg-Strelitz. 'Dearest Dad,' she wrote, 'I am absolutely crazy with excitement' at the prospect of the visit.[74] On 29 June she and her husband were staying at Hohenzieritz; Friedrich Wilhelm wrote his signature and the date on an interior wooden door. But the next day Luise felt unwell and did not get out of bed. The stress of war, as well as ten pregnancies in fifteen years, had taken their toll on her health. She was frequently ill, suffering from chest pains and chest infections. She probably had a heart complaint, and the curator at Hohenzieritz suggested that she may have suffered from a collapsed lung.

Her illness didn't seem to be too serious, so Friedrich Wilhelm returned to Berlin as scheduled. But Luise developed pneumonia, and over the following days her condition worsened. It seems to me that in history doctors often played down the severity of the illnesses of their royal patients; perhaps they did not want to take responsibility for bad news. This was the case with Luise's illness. Calming and hopeful reports were sent to her husband until, by 18 July, the doctors could temporise no longer, and Friedrich Wilhelm was called to come urgently to her bedside.

The bad news hit him hard. Friedrich Wilhelm was a hesitant and diffident man who depended heavily on his wife. He always felt his life was not favoured by fortune. Before he left for her bedside he wrote 'I am devastated by the most terrible of all anxieties,...Surely God, the

Almighty, will not deal with me so harshly again, for all my happiness hangs in the balance now.'[75]

He drove through the night to his dying wife with their two eldest sons, Fritz and Wilhelm, aged fourteen and thirteen. Both would become kings of Prussia and, as an old man, Wilhelm would be the emperor of a new German Empire. The trio arrived at Hohenzieritz at five o'clock on the morning of 19 July and walked from the village to avoid curious spectators. Luise comforted her husband and when he broke down sobbing, she urged him not to make a scene. She remained calm almost to the end, despite her suffering. Queen Luise of Prussia died at nine o'clock that same morning. One week later, her father found a piece of paper on his desk that his daughter had written a month earlier:

My dear father! I am so happy today as Your daughter and wife of the Best of all husbands![76]

Luise's body was brought back in slow stages from Hohenzieritz to Berlin. To mark the route, monuments were later erected at the places on the way where her coffin had rested. Thousands turned out to see it arrive in Berlin, where it temporarily rested for six months in the cathedral. On 23 December 1810, the first anniversary of her return from exile, Luise's body was interred in the newly built mausoleum at Charlottenburg. Luise had been popular with the Prussian people and, after her death, her legend would grow so that she would become the most famous queen of Prussia. She died young and was remembered for her youth and beauty, but she was also remembered for her courageous behaviour when her country was invaded. The elderly Field Marshal Blücher of Prussia was one of her greatest admirers. When he entered Paris in 1815, following Napoleon's final defeat, he is said to have cried out, 'Now, at last, Louise has been avenged!'[77]

Hohenzieritz suffered great neglect in the communist years but has been renovated and is now used as offices for the headquarters of the Muritz National Park. The wonderful landscape garden created by Karl and his English gardener has also been restored and is open to the public. The garden they designed can still be clearly recognised, with a large central meadow surrounded by a woodland belt, crisscrossed with paths and dotted with small lakes.[78] A short walk away from the schloss is the Temple of Luise, built by Karl in memory of his daughter in her favourite place in the garden. In the centre of this on a pedestal, is a head-and-shoulders statue of Luise, apparently modelled on her death mask. Her husband had a time capsule buried at the base of the pedestal with various items in memory of his wife.[79]

26. The room at Hohenzieritz where Queen Luise of Prussia died (aged only thirty-four) is now a fascinating small museum.

It was the room where Luise died that we had come to see at Hohenzieritz. The Königin Louise-Gedenkstätte (or Queen Luise memorial) is a small museum inside the schloss. Her father established the room in 1813 as a shrine to her memory and it was open on special anniversaries, such as her birthday and the date of her death. Everything was lost, however, along with all the contents of the schloss, at the end of World War II when the Russian army advanced and the area became part of the Soviet Occupied Zone. But thanks to the efforts of a private society called the Schlossvereins Hohenzieritz Louisen-Gedenskätte e.V. (Association of the Queen Louise Death Place at Hohenzieritz), the museum reopened in 2000, and the room where Luise died is again a memorial to her. There is also an exhibition about her in the schloss cavalier house.

There were no signs to the death room, so we wandered across the courtyard to the schloss and asked some of the office workers. They directed us up the steps and through the main entrance to a door on the left. This was locked but when the curator arrived after a few minutes, we entered an Aladdin's cave. This fascinating museum has three rooms; the first two are small anterooms to the death chamber and are packed full of paintings, photographs, porcelain, medals, and other memorabilia of Luise and her family. There is no space for a ticket office or even a desk or chair for the curator. The death chamber itself is the third room and has been restored to how it was before 1945. There is a copy of the funeral statue of Luise from the mausoleum at Charlottenburg, and several memorial wreaths.

For me, the most touching item in the museum was the old wooden door, which had been signed by Friedrich Wilhelm III. It must have been a tradition for visitors to do this, as there were also other royal signatures. But when Friedrich Wilhelm added his on 29 June 1810, before he returned to Berlin, he would have had no idea that in three weeks' time his wife would be dead.

Residenz Neustrelitz

The schloss at Neustrelitz was the home of a British princess for seventy-four years. She was Princess Augusta of Cambridge, the cousin of Queen Victoria, and she came here in 1843 when she married Prince Friedrich Wilhelm of Mecklenburg-Strelitz, the son and heir of the reigning grand duke. It was another grand match for the small principality.

When Mecklenburg-Strelitz was created in 1701, the new dukes initially lived in the small existing schloss in the town of Strelitz. But when this burnt down in 1712 the second duke, Adolf Friedrich III, decided to build a grand new palace, and indeed an entire new town, on the site of his hunting lodge three miles away on the bank of the Zierker See (lake). In doing so he was following the fashion of the time among German dukes, who all wanted to build an imitation of Versailles, the vast palace outside Paris built by the French Sun King, Louis XIV. For nineteen years the duke and his court had to 'camp out' in different buildings until the new schloss at Neustrelitz was completed in 1731.

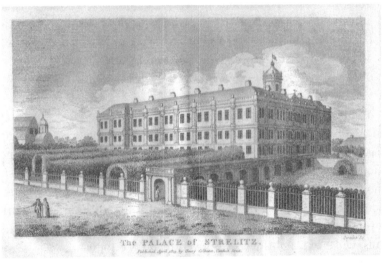

27. The grand palace at Neustrelitz was built in imitation of Versailles.

A new town was built adjacent to the palace with a unique ground plan of a star with eight avenues radiating from the central marketplace, like the spokes of a wheel. One of these, Schlossstrasse, leads to the palace and another, Seestrasse, to the lake. The duke gave ten-year tax exemptions to the duchy's nobility to encourage them to move to the new town. It was called Neustrelitz (new Strelitz), and the old town became Alt-Strelitz (or old Strelitz) to distinguish it.

The schloss was still relatively new when Queen Charlotte's brother became the duke and her family moved here from Mirow. In an old book I found a description of Schloss Neustrelitz as it was in 1766. Situated on high ground with formal baroque gardens sloping down to the lake behind and a parade ground and deer park in front, the schloss was 120 feet long and three stories high, with two wings sixty feet long projecting at right angles to form a large courtyard.

From the back gate of the palace you descend by a handsome flight of stone steps into the garden, where the eye is immediately presented with a charming landscape. Before you is a beautiful parterre [formal garden with beds in a symmetrical pattern] leading to a double row of trees, which form the grand avenue:...with a gradual slope to the edge of a spacious lake,...On the right side of the garden is the orangery....On the left is a kitchen garden.[80]

You can still stand on the same spot and see much the same view today. And it certainly would not have changed much when, eighty years after Queen Charlotte left her home to get married, her granddaughter, Augusta of Cambridge, arrived as a bride in 1843. Augusta, who was known in the family as Gussie, was the first cousin of Queen Victoria and three years younger. Edward, Duke of Kent (the fourth son of George III) was the father of Victoria and his brother Adolphus, Duke of Cambridge (the seventh son) of Augusta. As a young, unmarried princess, Gussie enjoyed being at the centre of attention at the court of the young Queen Victoria, but this came to an end when, aged twenty, she married Fritz Strelitz (Duke Friedrich Wilhelm of Mecklenburg-Strelitz).[81]

Their wedding in London, which was attended by Queen Victoria, almost descended into farce because of pushing and shoving over precedence among some of the guests. Victoria wanted her husband, Prince Albert of Saxe-Coburg, to rank immediately after her, but other British royals regarded him as a pushy upstart and thought he should only have the precedence he was due as a minor German duke. The elderly King Ernst August of Hannover, who was the uncle of both Victoria and Augusta, tried to elbow his way forward to be next to the queen herself. He was almost pushed over by Albert in his determination not to give up his place. More jostling followed over the order of signing the register and the procession into the celebration dinner.[82]

Duchess Augusta of Mecklenburg-Strelitz had a long life, and most of it was spent in Germany. Her life spanned five British reigns, from George IV to George V. She was always proud to have been born a British princess and kept up close links with the British royal family. She was passionate about politics and an ardent Tory (conservative). She felt far from the centre of things in provincial Neustrelitz and kept a home in London, which she visited every year until she was too old to make the journey anymore. This was Mecklenburg House in Buckingham Gate, just around the corner from Buckingham Palace. Today, quite appropriately, it is the home of the German-British Chamber of Commerce.

Augusta became an indomitable figure who saw her husband go blind, her country emasculated by Prussia, and her grandchildren engulfed by scandal. Her teenaged granddaughter Marie (the elder daughter of Augusta's only child, Adolphus Friedrich V) became pregnant by a footman and gave birth to an illegitimate daughter in 1898. Marie had probably been kept in total ignorance of the facts of life, as most princesses were until they married. Unfortunately it all became public knowledge when the footman, who had been dismissed for theft, took a case for unfair dismissal.[83] Marie's parents would have nothing more to do with her, but her grandmother stood by her.

Augusta took her granddaughter away to Mecklenburg House in London, to try to find a husband.[84] Marie married Count Jametel in 1899, but he turned out to be a poor choice. Jametel had married her only for her money and used his marriage to cloak a long-standing affair. Marie's husband was so unkind to her that in 1908 her younger brother, Karl Borwin, challenged him to a duel. The tragedy culminated in the death of nineteen-year-old Karl Borwin as a result.[85]

Augusta herself died in Neustrelitz, aged ninety-four, in December 1916, in the middle of the terrible war that split Europe's royal families. Brother and sister, nephew and uncle, and niece and aunt found themselves on opposite sides in the conflict. Augusta was isolated from her British relatives, but she managed to send a message to the British king, George V, to 'tell the King it is a stout old English heart that is ceasing to beat.'[86]

George V was married to Queen Mary (known as May in the family), who was the daughter of Augusta's sister, Mary Adelaide, Duchess of Teck. Queen Mary was always close to her aunt, who treated her as a daughter and influenced her life view.

There is a vivid pen picture of Duchess Augusta in James Pope-Hennessy's biography of Queen Mary. In this he describes her as short and plump and having the look of a complacent partridge.[87] He also gives a brilliantly evocative description of May's childhood visits to the old-fashioned court at Neustrelitz to see her aunt. The family would travel by train to Berlin, where they would be met by the grand duke's carriage for the final part of the journey, north across the sandy plains of Brandenburg. When they reached the border of Mecklenburg-Strelitz they would stop briefly for the grand duke's own horses to be harnessed, and then, with postilions and footmen in full livery (a postilion rides the left of a pair of carriage horses and you can still see them in British ceremonial processions today), they would drive the final miles and make their entry to Neustrelitz.

As the carriage clattered into the cobbled courtyard of the schloss, the band would start to play as the signal for their arrival, and 'the whole grand ducal court, stiff as a set of clockwork figures, would begin to take up their correct positions for the formal reception.' They would all be in full evening dress, whatever the time of day, the women wearing jewels and the men their medals and decorations. As the visitors entered the schloss, the doors to the reception room would be flung open, and 'a general obsequious motion of curtseying and bowing swept through the static group of courtiers like wind through the corn.'

The sisters, who were both demonstrative, 'would fall emotionally into one another's arms.'[88]

Fritz Strelitz and Gussie became grand duke and duchess in 1860 and reigned for forty-four years. When Fritz died in 1904, he was succeeded by their son Adolphus Friedrich V and when he died ten years later, on the eve of the outbreak of World War I, by their grandson Adolphus Friedrich VI, who would be the last grand duke of Mecklenburg-Strelitz.

28. The site of the palace is still a beautiful spot; view from the lake up through the gardens to where Schloss Neustrelitz once stood.

The last grand duke was the older brother of Karl Borwin, who had died as a result of the duel defending his sister Marie's honour. On the evening of 23 February 1918 Adolphus Friedrich VI, who was thirty-six, went for a walk with his dog and did not return. After a search his body was found the next morning in the icy waters of the Kammmerkanal, a nearby canal. The last grand duke had committed suicide by shooting himself. The reasons for his suicide have never been clearly established, and we can never know for sure what caused him such despair that he put a bullet through his temple. His suicide was during World War I, and there were rumours at the time that he could have been an English spy. The grand duke was English in his outlook and had been close to his English grandmother, Augusta, but it seems unlikely that he was a traitor. Another theory is that he felt under pressure to make an arranged marriage and father an heir, when he was already romantically involved with an actress, or he may even have made a morganatic marriage with her.[89]

The last grand duke died leaving no direct heirs. The succession was not clear so his distant cousin, Duke Friedrich Franz IV of Mecklenburg-Schwerin, became regent until the war ended later in the year, when the monarchy was abolished.

The schloss at Neustrelitz has not survived until the present day. Because of its remote location, it came through most of World War II unscathed but was then badly damaged in an arson attack, along with other parts of the town, in the final days of the war. The remains were demolished in 1950. The site and some of the secondary buildings are, however, still there. We stood in what would have been the entrance courtyard at the front of the schloss, with the palace church to our right and the gates to the deer park behind us. In front of us, the central axis of the baroque gardens still sloped down to the lake in the distance, with the orangery on the left, as it did in Grand Duchess Augusta's day. On the shore at the end of the vista was a garden folly, the Temple of Hebe, named after the Greek goddess of youth. This was built by Augusta's father-in-law, Grand Duke Georg, who was Queen Luise's brother.

Our visit to Neustrelitz was on a lovely day in May with the sun shining and the lilac in full bloom in the little park in front of the schloss church. This is now a gallery and music venue and was showing a scuplture exhibition while we were there. The site of the palace at the side of the lake is still a beautiful spot. We asked locally if there were any plans to rebuild the schloss and were told there was no money to do this. But the historic town centre of Neustrelitz was not damaged in the arson attack and the market square, with its eight radiating avenues, is still there. We had coffee and cakes in a very smart coffee shop in the square called Café Kowalewski. Our table had a glass top and there, under the glass, was a display of memorabilia about Queen Luise of Prussia, showing that she is not forgotten in Mecklenburg-Strelitz, even today.

Kaffee und Kuchen

Having a break for coffee and cakes (kaffee und kuchen) is almost an institution in Germany. Every morning, and often in the afternoon as well, you will see the cafés full of people chatting away while drinking coffee and eating the most delicious-looking cakes. My husband and I tried to avoid joining in at first, as we try to eat healthily, but very soon our resolve faltered and we gave up the fight. After that we would sometimes skip lunch in favour of this delicious German habit. We decided that it could not do too much harm just for a three-week trip.

Our tip to find the best cakes is to head to the local bakery, or bäckerei in German. Every village has one and they are open every day, even for a few hours on public holidays. They usually serve coffee and always have a mouth-watering display of fresh baked cakes. Or, if you prefer somewhere smarter, then look out for a café konditorei (café and pastry shop) like Café Kowalewski in Neustrelitz, as these will have an even larger and more elaborate display.

So when you are in Germany, I suggest you give kaffee und kuchen a try. The cream cakes were very popular, but my favourite was apfelkuchen— a cake with apples that was available in a local variation everywhere. I also enjoyed the deceptively plain-looking but absolutely gorgeous butterkuchen, or butter cake.

Burg Stargard

Our final visit in the area was to the fortified medieval castle at Burg Stargard, which is the oldest secular (non-church) building in Mecklenburg-Pomerania. We went with absolutely no expectations about what it would be like, since we had seen only a brief description in a local brochure. We were in for a very pleasant surprise and from the moment we walked into the cobbled internal courtyard of the schloss, shaded with flowering chestnut trees, this was a favourite schloss.

Burg Stargard was built in the middle of the thirteenth century by the Margraves of Brandenburg, who also at that time held the lordship of Stargard. Both the lordship and the burg came to Mecklenburg in 1292, as part of the dowry of Princess Beatrix of Brandenburg when she married Duke Heinrich II of Mecklenburg. When Beatrix died the ownership was disputed, but Mecklenburg managed to hold onto its new possession. Over the following centuries Burg Stargard would be first a residence for the dukes of the separate principality of Mecklenburg-Stargard, then part of Mecklenburg-Schwerin, and finally, from 1701, part of the newly created Mecklenburg-Strelitz.

The burg has a lovely position, on a hilltop and surrounded by open countryside. In good weather there is a thirty-kilometre view from the top of the belfry tower. It is built of brick and is a fine example of the Brick Gothic style of architecture, which is found around the Baltic Sea from Sweden through Denmark, Germany, and Poland and as far as the Baltic states of Lithuania, Latvia, and Estonia. This historic style of architecture is a legacy of the powerful Hanseatic League of cities, which dominated trade in this region in the Middle Ages. Brick was commonly used as a building material in northern Germany, where stone is scarce, and it was humbling to think that the thousands and thousands of bricks used at Burg Stargard were all made by hand. The burg was described in the brochure as an 'impressive brick colossus'[90].

Burg Stargard is a group of buildings, and it has the feeling of a country village rather than a grand palace. We started in the outer ward of the castle where there are the old stables (now the town museum), the old prison (now a small hotel), and the barn (now the café). From there, a path took us uphill and through the narrow arched entrance of the Third Upper Gate to the inner ward and the part of the schloss that we liked the best—a cobbled courtyard with tall chestnut trees in the centre. These were in flower when we were there. This circular courtyard is enclosed by a ring of historic buildings, the outside walls of which form the fortifications of the burg. Some of the buildings are preserved intact and others are in ruins. All of them had information boards, which happily were all translated into English, so we were able to find out about the history of Burg Stargard.

29. Burg Stargard is a fine example of the Brick Gothic style of architecture, which is found around the Baltic Sea.

The Krummes Haus, or Crooked House, is one of the oldest buildings, and it dates in part from about 1245. This is where the last trial

30. The Burg is the oldest secular building in Mecklenburg.

for witchcraft in Mecklenburg took place in 1726. The Krummes Haus was destroyed by arson on 18 December 1819, but its reconstruction is now in the planning phase. Farther around the courtyard is the Alten Münze, or the Old Mint, which dates from 1250. This gets its name from the years in the 1740s when it was the Mecklenburg-Strelitz mint, producing coins for Duke Adolphus Friedrich III. It burnt down in 1893 and was eventually rebuilt as an inn in 1938, which is how it is used again today. On the other side of the courtyard is what's left of the Residence, or Duke's Palace, which was pulled down in 1720 to provide building material for the new palace at Neustrelitz. And next to this is the Ladies' Wing, built in 1352 to provide accommodation for the duke's family and the ladies of the court. Later used also as a prison, it was struck by lightning and burnt down in 1792, so only part remains.

We had a most enjoyable morning wandering about the pretty courtyard and learning about the history of these buildings, which goes back over 750 years. After the abolition of the monarchy, the town of Burg Stargard bought the schloss in 1926 and carried out some restoration work, including the rebuilding of the Old Mint. The situation changed again at the end of World War II, and during the GDR years the schloss was used as accommodation for a National Youth School (Landesjugendschule) and later a youth hostel. Since the reunification of Germany in 1990 there has been more restoration work, and even more is planned. Burg Stargard is now a monument open to the public, and it also houses a hotel, restaurant (inn), wedding venue, and museum. It also has our favourite schloss café of the entire tour.

This is housed in the barn, which dates from 1700 and was previously used as a granary. It's part of the farm buildings in the outer ward, which gives the café a distinct rustic feel. We sat on wooden benches placed on the brick-and-stone floor of the barn, with the big doors at both ends open and the sun shining in. The coffee machine was tucked away on the counter of the gift shop next door, and the cake appeared from a plastic storage box underneath this. Both were excellent. Outside the barn there is a carefully tended herb-and-wild-flower garden. The waitress was picking flowers from this and arranging them in jam jars for the café tables. Vines are also grown in the small farmyard. It was a spring day in a lovely country place, and we came away from Burg Stargard feeling very happy.

31. The rustic café in the barn at Burg Stargard was
our favourite of the tour.

Schloss Blücher—Three Times Restored in the Twentieth Century

The Mecklenburg Lake District was a favourite spot for the Mecklenburg nobility to build schlösser. One of them was Schloss Blücher at Göhren-Lebbin, near Lake Fleesensee. This is now the Radisson Blu Resort Hotel, where we stayed.

Schloss Blücher was built in the 1840s by a descendant of the famous Field Marshal Blücher who, although holding a senior rank in the Prussian army, came from Mecklenburg. It was Blücher's arrival on the field at Waterloo, late in the afternoon, that caused Napoleon to lose his last battle. The elderly field marshal, who was in his seventies, had insisted on bringing his troops up despite being wounded earlier that day.

The schloss did not stay long in the ownership of the Blücher family; in 1871 it was sold to a wealthy industrialist. His family saved the schloss after it burned down in 1912; they restored it in a different, neo-Gothic, style. But after World War I they too moved on, and eventually the schloss became a school. At the end of World War II it served as a military hospital and a home for refugees. Later in the GDR years, it housed apartments, as well as a doctor's surgery, post office, shop, and kindergarten. The schloss was poorly maintained and the fabric of the building deteriorated considerably.

Schloss Blücher was restored for the second time in the 1970s to become a holiday home for employees of the state-owned East German recycling company called VEB SERO. Its purpose was to save the scarce foreign-currency resources of the GDR by recycling to cut down raw material imports. The third restoration was in the 1990s, after the fall of the GDR and the reunification of Germany. In 2000 the schloss opened as a hotel and today is at the centre of a thriving holiday area—Land Fleesensee—with a marina, a golf course, cycling trails and tennis courts. Even today the schloss still has the lingering feeling of its time in the seventies and eighties as an institutional holiday camp—with long corridors, utilitarian furniture, and a vast dining hall.

But it is a very nice place to stay, and my husband and I enjoyed our time there.

5

BRANDENBURG AND THE HOHENZOLLERNS

The Mecklenburg Lake District was the farthest point east on our tour. From there, we would turn and head west again. But before we did, the opportunity to make a short detour into neighbouring Brandenburg to see the schloss at Rheinsberg was too good to miss. This was the home, in turn, of two talented brothers from the Hohenzollern royal family. Here we would find a schloss they both loved, and also unravel their story of sibling rivalry.

Rheinsberg is located in the far north of Brandenburg, and a forty-mile journey from our hotel in Göhren-Lebbin did not seem too far for a day trip by car. However it turned out to be quite an adventure, as we had not reckoned on the roads! In Germany these are generally excellent and it is apparent that in what was East Germany, there has been a lot of recent investment in the infrastructure of the roads. But once we turned off the major road our route went across country, and it was quite a different situation. The road was narrow, rough, and covered with potholes. The road surface was a patchwork of old repairs, and in many places there were patches on top of previous patches. In some places the road reverted to old fashioned cobbles.

We bumped along slowly for mile after mile, as it was impossible to go faster. The worst sections were going through the villages where there was no road at all. It simply stopped at the entrance to a village and started again at the exit. Within the village the road was little more than a cart track. When we asked later, we were told this was because the money for road repairs in the villages comes from a different budget. It all seemed rather unreal and it was like going back in time. It was a relief when we reached Rheinsberg and normality.

Rheinsberg

Schloss Rheinsberg was the home where Frederick the Great (King Friedrich II of Prussia), and later his younger brother Prince Heinrich, found happiness and contentment. The schloss is built on an island in the Grienericksee Lake and connected to the shore by three bridges—one leading to the main entrance, one to the cavalier house, and one to the schloss gardens. The front of the schloss looks plain and utilitarian, with rather ugly, oversized corner pavilions. But when we walked through the central arch and into the inner courtyard, it just took our breath away. On either side a slender wing protrudes forward towards the lake, ending in a small round tower. And connecting the two wings, to make up the fourth side of the courtyard, is an elegant, open colonnade. The courtyard is full of air and light. I almost felt I was flying. And through the colonnade is a glorious view across the lake to the far shore where, central to the vista, is an obelisk. This was put up by Heinrich after the death of Frederick, almost to spite his brother.

To understand the relationship between Frederick the Great and his brother Heinrich, we first of all have to go back to the story of Frederick and his father. A characteristic of the Hohenzollern kings was their inability to get along with their eldest sons and heirs. The conflict between Frederick and his father was by no means the first example of this. Frederick's grandfather and great grandfather had both fallen out

32. Schloss Rheinsberg was the home where Frederick the Great of Prussia and later his younger brother, Prince Heinrich, found happiness and contentment.

with their fathers and fled abroad in the belief that their lives were threatened. The pattern was repeated with Frederick.

Frederick said that the four years he spent at Rheinsberg were the happiest of his life.[91] The schloss was a haven for him, away from the controlling influence of his father, where he could pursue his interests in music, literature, and the arts with an amenable circle of friends. Before coming to Rheinsberg Frederick had endured years of conflict with his father, culminating in an abortive attempt to run away, following which he was arrested and imprisoned. Rheinsberg was part of his rehabilitation.

Frederick's father was King Friedrich Wilhelm I of Prussia. He was a difficult man to live with and a tyrant to his family. He expected his son to grow up in his own image, displaying the (what we now think of as Prussian) virtues of frugality, discipline, and military prowess. In later years, Frederick did in fact show all of these and would have made his father very proud. But the young Frederick was also interested in very different things—he wanted to write poetry, play the flute, and read novels. The more his father tried to force him to conform, the more Frederick learnt to hide his interests and carry them on in secret. When he was twelve years old, his father said,

> I would like to know what is going on in this little head,...I know for sure that he does not think as I do.[92]

Friedrich Wilhelm had a very short temper and resorted to physical punishment of his son. He was a Hanoverian on his mother's side and possibly suffered (like his relative George III) from the hereditary disease of porphyria, meaning that he was often in pain and sometimes mentally unbalanced.[93] Goaded by his son's silent refusal to be what he wanted him to be, Friedrich Wilhelm would beat and humiliate him in public. Then he would taunt his son that he was a coward and that he would have run away had his own father done the same to him.[94]

When Frederick was eighteen years old, in 1730, he could take no more and decided to escape from Prussia. With the help of a friend, he planned to ride off in the middle of the night while on a trip away from Berlin with his father. But they were hopeless plotters, and inevitably their plans were discovered; Frederick was arrested while attempting to get away. Friedrich Wilhelm's retribution was terrible. To him Frederick had committed the most grievous offence: he was an officer in the Prussian army who had deserted his post and was guilty of treason. He wrote to his wife that

> I no longer acknowledge him for my son. He has dishonoured me and my house. Such a wretch does not deserve to live.[95]

He was dissuaded from executing Frederick, but his vengeance fell on those he thought had aided his son. Frederick was close to his elder sister Wilhelmine, and in her memoirs she talks about her fear of what the king would do and how she and her mother broke into Frederick's desk to burn incriminating letters. She describes how on his return home, her father became violent.

> He grew black, his eyes sparkled with rage, and he foamed at the mouth. '*Infamous baggage!*' said he to me, '*dare you show yourself before me? Go and keep company with your rascally brother.*' In uttering these words, he seized me with one hand, and struck me several times in the face with his fist.[96]

Wilhelmine's punishment was to be forced to choose between two minor German princes for a husband. She had expected to make a much grander match but was told that the life of her brother could depend on her bowing to the king's will. She chose, and married the margrave of Bayreuth.

The friend who had helped Frederick, Hans Hermann von Katte, was condemned to death by the king. He was beheaded in the courtyard of Küstrin fortress, where Frederick was imprisoned, while his jailors held his face to the window to force him to watch. When he realised his friend would die because of him, Frederick had begged his father to spare von Katte or to kill him instead. Afterwards he submitted entirely, enduring the terms of his imprisonment without complaint and doing everything his father wanted. Gradually the terms of his confinement were eased, and he was rehabilitated. In 1733, against his own inclination, he married the bride of his father's choice—Princess Elisabeth Christine of Brunswick-Wolfenbüttel. A year later, the king bought Rheinsberg for the young couple.

Frederick's treatment at the hands of his father must have left him with deep psychological scars, so it is surprising, or perhaps it is not, that he handed out some of the same treatment to his brothers. Frederick had three, all much younger than he was (please see chart 10). Heinrich, who was the middle of the three, was fourteen years younger than Frederick and was fourteen years old when Friedrich Wilhelm died. He was the most like Frederick and always jealous of his elder

33. Statue of Frederick the Great outside the gates at Rheinsberg.

brother's position. He chafed under Frederick's authoritarian control and as he grew older tried to get away by asking for permission to leave Prussia and serve in a foreign army, which was refused.[97]

Heinrich wanted to have an independent establishment of his own, but the only way Frederick would permit this was if his brother got married. So in 1752 Heinrich, who was probably gay,[98] married Wilhelmine of Hesse-Kassel as the price of getting Rheinsberg. Like his brother he married under pressure and for the wrong reasons, and like Frederick, he later repudiated his wife. As soon as he came to the throne, Frederick separated from Elisabeth Christine, who was condemned to a shadow life in her own schloss at Schönhausen. As soon as he had reason to do so (there were rumours of her having an affair), Heinrich did the same and Wilhelmine was banished from Rheinsberg to live separately in Berlin. There were no children from either marriage, and it is possible that neither was consummated.

The real trouble between the brothers dated from the Seven Years' War and the aftermath of the Prussian defeat at the Battle of Kolin in June 1757. Frederick was fast becoming a great general, and he relied upon his equally talented brother as his second-in-command. Later he would say that Heinrich was the 'only General in the Seven Years' War who never slipped up.'[99] But the brother who was between them in age, August Wilhelm, did make a mistake during the retreat from the battle, at the cost of men and equipment. Frederick turned upon him, stripped him of his command, and practically accused him of cowardice. A year later, August Wilhelm was dead of a stroke.

The Hohenzollers

The House of Hohenzollern took its name from their ancestral seat, Schloss Hohenzollern, near Stuttgart in the south German state of Baden-Württemberg. In the twelfth century the family split into two, and it was the junior of the two lines (known simply as the Hohenzollern) who would eventually become emperors of Germany and to whom Frederick and Heinrich belong.

The Hohenzollerns were burgraves of Nuremburg until 1417, when they purchased the Mark of Brandenburg from the Holy Roman emperor and moved north. Brandenburg was just a frontier province of the Holy Roman Empire and relatively poor, but it had one valuable asset—an electoral vote. The new elector of Brandenburg became one of only seven German princes with the right to elect the Holy Roman emperor.

The principle of primogeniture was established early with the Hohenzollerns (in the fifteenth century), so they did not suffer the disadvantage that most other noble German families did of seeing the family inheritance diminished by dividing it among sons. In the early seventeenth century, their lands were increased through marriage when the duchy of Prussia and some small duchies along the Rhine passed to the current elector as the inheritance of his wife. Prussia was outside the Holy Roman Empire (and the jurisdiction of the emperor), and this enabled the electors of Brandenburg to be promoted to kings. From 1701 they became kings of Prussia.

The new possessions were detached from Brandenburg (Prussia to the east and the Rhine duchies to the west), and this would drive the policy of Hohenzollern electors and kings. They were unanimous in their determination to defend what they had and to add to it by joining their scattered lands. This was achieved bit by bit until, after the victory over Austria in the Seven Weeks' War of 1866, Prussia stretched from the Netherlands to Poland. In his wonderful book, Christopher Clark includes a section of six maps that show this expansion in a nutshell and encapsulate the history of Prussia.[100]

Defeat in the Seven Weeks' War ended the influence of Austria in German affairs and left Prussia predominant. In 1871 the king of Prussia was proclaimed as emperor of a new German empire by the other German princes.

Heinrich never forgave Frederick for disgracing August Wilhelm and wrote to their other brother, Ferdinand, that 'all my life I shall carry this consuming poison with me.'[101] Whatever honours Frederick later gave him, Heinrich never forgot the treatment of August Wilhelm. All his life he resented coming second to Frederick, and perhaps he also realised that he too might be dispensable should he make a mistake. After Frederick's death in 1786, Heinrich erected the obelisk at Rheinsberg as a memorial to the heroes of the Seven Years' War. The name of one brother, August Wilhelm, is given pride of place. The name of another, Frederick the Great, is pointedly omitted altogether.[102]

Heinrich redesigned the interiors at Rheinsberg and made many other changes at the schloss, including developing the gardens and building those two corner pavilions that I found ugly. Inside the rooms have elegant proportions but are quite small, more like a comfortable country home than a grand palace. Prince Heinrich's private rooms are on the first floor overlooking the garden, and underneath these on the ground floor he had a second set for use in summer so he could walk directly out into it. It was in these summer rooms that he died in August 1802. He was at his happiest at Rheinsberg, where he lived for fifty years until his death.

The largest room at Rheinsberg, where the décor survives from Frederick's time at the schloss, is the Hall of Mirrors which takes up the whole of the width of the slender northern wing. The light comes flooding through the windows on three sides of the room and is magnified by the mirrors, which also reflect the glittering surface of the lake outside. With the ceiling above painted as the sky and the shimmering mirrors, it almost feels as if the floor is part of the lake. I could easily imagine Frederick making music in this room.

After Heinrich's death Rheinsberg was never again used as a royal residence. The schloss was inherited by the youngest and only surviving brother, Ferdinand, and most of the contents were sold off at a series of auctions. Even today, after restoration, it is still mostly bare of furniture and other contents. By the end of the nineteenth century

34. Frederick the Great as crown prince with his three younger brothers; Heinrich is on the right.

the empty schloss had acquired a romantic image with German artists and writers and, inspired by their works, Rheinsberg became a tourist destination. After World War II it suffered a similar fate to so many other schlösser behind the Iron Curtain. Rheinsberg was turned into a sanatorium and, during the next forty years, it underwent considerable damage as the interiors were altered to suit its new use and many original features were lost. When restoration began in 1991, after German reunification, some of the original doors were discovered being used locally as a coal shed!

Rheinsberg has the atmospheric feeling of a lost age and is a wonderful place to visit. It was well worth that bumpy journey over pot-holed roads to see it. Our visit was enhanced by a good audio guide commentary which brought the history of the schloss to life with, for example, quotes from Heinrich's letters. Rheinsberg will always be associated with the two brothers who, in turn, found a haven here. Frederick and Heinrich were very alike, and part of their personal tragedy was that they never really understood each other.

6

THURINGIA AND THE WETTIN AND SCHWARZBURG-RUDOLSTADT FAMILIES

The state of Thuringia is unknown Germany for most Britons; I had hardly heard of it before we started visiting schlösser. Much of its picturesque countryside is covered by the Thüringer Wald (or Thuringian Forest) and this, together with the state's location right in the centre of the country, is the reason why Thuringia is often called the Green Heart of Germany. After spending time there I can say that Thuringia is, in my opinion, the most beautiful part of what is undoubtedly a very beautiful country.

Thuringia is one of the smallest and least populated of Germany's federal states, so it was surprising to learn that before World War I it was split into seven even smaller duchies and principalities. This multitude of royal families means that Thuringia has more schlösser per square mile than anywhere else in Germany. Here, we would find a schloss that was coveted by Hitler and a tiny court that became the centre of European culture, and we would discover more about the ancestry of Prince George of Cambridge.

Saalfeld

At Saalfeld, we received the best welcome of any of the schlösser we visited. Our expectations for the visit were not high, as we knew that the schloss is not a museum but is used as local government offices. But as we parked the car we bumped into two ladies who worked there, and they urged us to visit the chapel, explaining it was open to the public that day.

35. The schloss at Saalfeld was built by the ancestor of
Prince George of Cambridge.

The schloss was built as the residence of the first duke of Saxe-Saal-feld. After the death of Duke Ernst the Pious of Gotha in 1675 there was a huge inheritance dispute between his seven sons, which lasted for several years. Eventually his lands were split into seven, to provide a principality for each of them, and the youngest son, Johann Ernest, became the first duke of the tiny duchy of Saxe-Saalfeld. Later on Coburg would be added, so the duchy became Saxe-Coburg-Saalfeld (please see chart 11 for a simplified history of the duchy).

The Wettins

The dukes of Saxe-Coburg-Saalfeld were part of the house of Wettin, which can trace its ancestry back to the tenth century and earlier. The Wettins were originally margraves of Meissen and in 1423 were made electors of Saxony by the Holy Roman emperor. From then on, the family took this as their senior title.

Like many other noble houses at that time, the Wettins were prone to dividing their lands between sons. In 1485 there was a lasting split when two brothers, Ernst and Albrecht, divided the house and its lands into two branches called the Ernestine and the Albertine. Ernst was the elder brother and retained the electorate of Saxony, and his younger brother Albrecht took the margraviate of Meissen.

However several generations later, the Ernestine branch lost Saxony to the Albertine. Ernst's descendant, Elector Johann Friedrich I, led a rebellion of the Protestant German princes against the Catholic Holy Roman emperor. He was defeated in 1547 at the Battle of Mühlberg, captured by the emperor, and forced to sign over the electorate to his cousin Maurice of the Albertine branch. Thereafter the Albertine (who are featured in Schloss I) were electors of Saxony and for a time also kings of Poland. The Ernestine branch became less important.

Over the following centuries the Ernestines went through further divisions and reorganisations, and from this branch were descended several royal families who ruled small states in Thuringia. Three of these are featured in this book. They all have triple-barrelled names, which I shall shorten for ease of reference as follows: Saxe-Coburg-Saalfeld (Saxe-Coburg), Saxe-Gotha-Altenburg (Saxe-Gotha), and Saxe-Weimar-Eisenach (Saxe-Weimar).

The schloss at Saalfeld was built in the new baroque style that came into fashion in Germany around the end of the Thirty Years' War (1618–1648). The new style reflected a change in the purpose of a prince's residence. In previous centuries, a schloss had been a fortified castle for defence against attack. Now it became a grand palace, with a suite of public staterooms intended for show and to impress. The baroque period lasted until around the end of the eighteenth century when it was succeeded by a new style, with more simple and less cluttered lines, called neoclassicism.

Saalfeld is small, with three wings in horseshoe pattern around an open courtyard, and painted in brown and cream. The chapel is in the left wing and entrance is through a plain wooden door over which was a banner declaring it to be 'Ein kleinod des Barock' (a jewel of the baroque). Even so, we were unprepared for the riot of elaborate decoration that lay inside.

I can only compare the chapel to a beautiful pink-and-white two-tiered wedding cake (the second tier being a gallery supported on slender pillars). It was inaugurated in 1720 with a family wedding, so perhaps the comparison is apt. Cherubs romp across the ceiling, paintings and intricate plasterwork cover the walls, and the whole room is lit by light from the windows on two levels all around. The focal point is a gorgeous grey alabaster altar with a painting of the Ascension reaching as high as the gallery. The pulpit is at gallery level above the altar and faces the duke's pew at the other end of the chapel. Rising above it all, behind the altar and the pulpit, is a magnificent silver organ that glitters in the sun. Saalfeld may be a small schloss but its chapel rivals anything we saw on our tour.

Across the courtyard from the chapel, in what was originally the Garden Hall of the schloss, is the *bürgerbüro* where the locals go to pay their motor tax. We decided to call in here, on the off chance that there might be some information about the history of the schloss. We got a wonderful welcome from the lady behind the desk who, recognising our interest, called up a colleague to come and talk to us. Martin works in local government but also turned out to be a fellow enthusiast for German royal history. He told us about the genealogy of Prince George of Cambridge and provided information about the history of the schloss, which his son very kindly later translated into English for me. Martin also took us on a personal tour of the building.

The schloss has been government offices since the 1920s, which is what has ensured its survival until today. But it does mean that the interior has been altered and much has been lost, notably the ballroom on the first floor. However, the main staircase as well as the chapel remains in its original form. Our tour included an adventurous trip up to the roof to see the views from the balcony around the clock tower. We climbed several flights of stairs and went along walkways through the attics where my husband, who loves old buildings, was enthralled by the original joinery some of which still showed signs of old fire damage.

Prince George of Cambridge, who was born in July 2013, is a direct descendant (the ten times great grandson) of Johann Ernst, the first duke of Saxe-Saalfeld (please see chart 12). This is why the town feels a special connection with the British royal family and celebrated his birth with articles in the newspapers and a special Prince George's Beer. The connection began in 1818 when Princess Victoire of Saxe-Coburg, the great, great granddaughter of Johann Ernst, married Edward Duke of Kent, the fourth son of George III. Their only child, born the following year, was Queen Victoria. The connection continued in the next generation when, in 1840, Victoria married her cousin Albert of Saxe-Coburg (the son of her mother's brother). But by now Saalfeld had gone to another branch of the family under a further reorganisation of Ernestine lands. This is the reason why Saalfeld's place in the ancestry of the British royal family is often overlooked and the town feels it is forgotten.

One of the sources I most enjoyed reading when researching for this book was the diary of Duchess Augusta of Saxe-Coburg (1757–1831), who was the second wife of Duke Franz Friedrich Anton (1750–1806). Duchess Augusta was a formidable woman, the mother of nine

36. In her diary, Duchess Augusta of Saxe-Coburg described how she watched the Battle of Saalfeld from the schloss windows.

children (two of whom died as children) and the grandmother of both Queen Victoria and Prince Albert. A book of extracts from her private diaries was published in 1941 by Victoria's youngest daughter, Beatrice, and I found it when browsing through the online catalogue of the London Library. Called *In Napoleonic Days*, the extracts cover the turbulent years of the Napoleonic Wars; when the book opens in April 1806, the French have occupied the German Rhineland, Austria has been defeated at the Battle of Austerlitz, and the Holy Roman empire is breaking up. These are Augusta's opening words:

> The moon shines cold and bright in a cloudless sky. The mild breath of Spring has given way to cold biting east winds. It seems as if nature had allied itself with humanity to destroy all thoughts of happiness. There are nothing but storms in the atmosphere

and among men. Poor Germany, what will thy fate yet be, given over to the caprices of a despot [Napoleon I], who recognises no law but his own will, who sets no limit to his own lust for power, and to whom all means are justifiable to gratify this passion.[103]

Later in the year, on October 2, Augusta writes her diary entry at Schloss Saalfeld, where the ducal household have fled (from their primary residence at Coburg) to avoid Napoleon's invading army. On 7 October, she records the safe arrival at Saalfeld of her daughter and son-in-law, Count and Countess Mensdorff-Pouilly. But it is a case of 'out of the frying pan and into the fire' because Saalfeld is also in the path of the advance, and on the morning of 10 October, the French clashed with Prussian troops within sight of the schloss. Augusta's diary tells how she watched the Battle of Saalfeld from the schloss windows and saw wave after wave of French troops streaming out of the woods and attacking the Prussians. 'The whole scene of bloodshed lay spread out before us....Their cavalry emerged from the forest and streamed along in a never-ending and terrifying procession....A terrible blood-curdling din was kept up by drums and bugles.'[104]

The Prussian troops were commanded by Prince Luis Ferdinand, who was a cousin of King Friedrich Wilhelm III of Prussia.[105] Luis Ferdinand was a bit of a renegade in the Prussian royal family; he had become frustrated by the king's approach to dealing with Napoleon and was keen to take on the French at the first opportunity. But he soon found himself outnumbered and outmanoeuvred at Saalfeld, and in the chaos of retreat he was killed in the hand-to-hand fighting. Count Mensdorff-Pouilly searched the battlefield until he found the prince's body and insisted that it be taken to the schloss.[106] I was spellbound as I read Augusta's account of how she saw it carried into the courtyard.

In the midst of the turmoil of departing and arriving officers, something drew me to the window to watch a warlike scene. A detachment of infantry with its eagles, preceded by bearded sappers, marched into the courtyard carrying something on poles. Only when they dropped their burden on the ground did I recognise the body of Prince Luis Ferdinand. Naked and only wrapped in a rough cloth, lay this great Prince, his fine head uncovered. No wound had disfigured his beautiful face. At the back of his head were some slight contusions, but in the bared breast yawned a deep wound, which had put an end to his life.[107]

The French were moving on and were going to leave the body where it was. It was only when Count Mensdorff-Pouilly shouted above the din that they must give last honours to a dead hero that they carried it into the chapel. It is sobering to think that the courtyard of the schloss, where we stood between the baroque chapel and the motor tax office, was once the scene of such events.

Mort du Prince de Prusse

37. Prince Luis Ferdinand was killed in hand-to-hand fighting at Saalfeld.

Over the following days, weeks, and months, Augusta's diary is a compelling account of the horrors of living in a war zone—of the immediate aftermath of the Battle of Saalfeld with the French in the schloss and the unburied bodies of men and horses lying on the battlefield; of the sacked and burning villages and destitute population; and of the local men and boys conscripted to fight and die for Napoleon who never returned home. The diary records personal tragedy too as, after his duchy's revenues are sequestered by Napoleon, Augusta's husband dies in December broken by the shock of events. But in later years it also records happier events, including the marriages of her children, which would be the start of the family's great rise in fortunes—but more of that at our next two schlösser.

Friedenstein

Friedenstein is an absolute monster of a schloss. Huge and white, it towers above the town of Gotha and is visible from miles around. A famous resident of Gotha once said that he lived in its shadow, and that the duke could use its two thousand windows to look down from the castle to the city and keep his eyes fixed on all his subjects.[108]

In 1641, towards the end of the Thirty Years' War, Duke Ernst I (Ernst the Pious) inherited the principality of Gotha. He found it in a pitiful condition, having suffered from fire, famine, and plague as well as constant troop movements through the little territory. He decided to build his residence there, and in 1643 the foundation stone of his new schloss was laid. It was the first castle to be built after the Thirty Years' War, and he called it Friedenstein, or Rock of Peace, to reflect hope for the future rather than the ravages of the past.

The schloss was built on the ruins of a previous castle at Gotha called Grimmenstein, which had been razed to the ground in 1567 on the orders of the Holy Roman emperor. Grimmenstein had been the residence of Johann Friedrich II, the son of the unfortunate Johann Friedrich I from the Ernestine branch of the Wettin family who had been forced to sign over the electorate of Saxony to the Albertines (see Schloss Saalfeld). His son was not much more fortunate. Johann Friedrich II made the mistake of sheltering an outlaw at Grimmenstein and refusing to give him up. Like his father before him, he was placed under the Imperial Ban by the emperor, which meant he lost all his rights and that his property could legally be taken from him by other princes. Of course, it was his cousin from the Albertine branch who took advantage of this. Elector Augustus of Saxony, who was the brother of the Elector Maurice who had dispossessed Johann Friedrich I, besieged Grimmenstein and then destroyed it. Johann Friedrich II spent the rest of his life in prison.

38. Friedenstein was the first castle to be built after the Thirty Years' War, and its name means Rock of Peace.

Friedenstein is built on a horseshoe pattern, with a central wing and two side wings that each end in a massive square tower. On the fourth side, the courtyard between the wings is enclosed by a single-story wall.

The schloss is so huge (the ground plan is 100 metres by 140 metres) that the courtyard is big enough for a military parade ground or several football pitches. One of the reasons for the schloss's size is that Ernst I was a believer in centralisation. So church, arsenal, mint, archives, stables, and all of the other institutions and services of his duchy were under the same roof as his residence. Ernst reigned for over thirty years and did much to rebuild Gotha after the ravages of war. In 1672 his wife's inheritance was added to increase his duchy's size, and it became Saxe-Gotha-Altenburg (Saxe-Gotha for short).

Ernst and his wife had seventeen children, and when he died in 1675 there were seven surviving sons. Ernst had intended them to rule jointly—the eldest as the duke and the others as a sort of cabinet of ministers.[109] But he failed to leave a will setting this out clearly, so (this being the Ernestine branch) a major fight erupted, with each son claiming an inheritance. The dispute went on for several years until eventually it was referred to the Holy Roman emperor in Vienna for arbitration. Perhaps it is not surprising that he came down in favour of splitting the father's lands to create a smaller duchy for each son—after all, it was not in the emperor's interests to have powerful vassals.[110] So this is how the sixth son of Ernst I became duke of a new duchy of Saxe-Saalfeld (see Schloss Saalfeld). Ernst's eldest surviving son became Duke Friedrich I of the new but smaller Saxe-Gotha.

Today Schloss Friedenstein is still a multipurpose building and home to two museums, the Public Records Office, university library, castle church, and the fascinating Ekhof Theatre, which dates from the baroque period and still has its original stage sets and machinery in good working order. We visited the Schloss Museum, which is itself enormous and houses numerous collections, from antiquities to contemporary art, as well as the state apartments. We followed the *rundgang* (suggested tour) but soon became lost in what seemed like an endless series of rooms. Also I lost the fight with the high-tech, touch-screen audio guide, which had to be reset for the different sections of the museum as well as changed from room to room. The whole experience was energy sapping. Fortunately our visit was saved by the wonderful museum attendants, who were among the friendliest and most helpful we found on all our schloss visits.

It started well in the ticket office, where a lady attendant took time

39. When Duke Ernst the Pious died his duchy was divided between his seven sons.

to talk me through key points in the history of the duchy and the family. As we walked around the museum smiling attendants untangled my audio guide, suggested where to go next, and even coped when we lost our photo permit. Best of all they helped me to identify the family portraits, many of which did not have labels. One was of Augusta of Saxe-Gotha, who made the first of the family's two great dynastic marriages with the British royal family when she married Frederick, Prince of Wales in 1736. Frederick died before his father, so Augusta never became queen of England, but she was the mother of George III and, according to the audio guide, the alliance with Britain helped protect the small duchy from invasion in the Seven Years' War.

The second of the great marriages was when Prince Albert married Queen Victoria in 1840. One of the reasons that I particularly wanted to go to Friedenstein was to find out more about Albert's mother, Luise of Saxe-Gotha, who was born there. Luise was divorced from Albert's father and separated from her children while still in her twenties, following a scandal about her love life. There are few portraits of her in existence, and the attendants helped me find two at Friedenstein that I had never seen before.

The Problem of Inheritance and Younger Sons

Before the eighteenth century, many of Germany's royal families did not follow primogeniture. This is a practice in which family property and titles are passed on to a single heir, usually the eldest son. The alternative is that the family inheritance is divided among several heirs, as we have seen when, after the death of Duke Ernst I of Saxe-Gotha, his lands were divided into seven to provide a duchy for each son.

The practice of primogeniture had advantages and disadvantages. The prime advantage was that family wealth, and therefore prestige, was kept intact rather than being diminished down the generations. After Duke Ernst August of Hannover broke with his family tradition and introduced primogeniture in the 1680s, he was able to use the combined family wealth to obtain the much-coveted rank of elector of the Holy Roman Empire. The downside of primogeniture was that it caused jealousy among siblings and left younger sons without any inheritance. Ernst August's decision caused great bitterness among his sons and fractured the family.

Given the high rates of child mortality, having several sons was desirable to ensure continuance of the family line. However, with primogeniture younger sons were without the prospect of an inheritance, so they usually had to remain unmarried and earn their own living. Many became soldiers of fortune (professional mercenaries) in foreign armies and died young in battle, as happened with three of the six sons of Ernst August.

In later centuries primogeniture became the usual rule. Many families introduced it during the eighteenth century—for example, Mecklenburg-Strelitz from 1701 and Saxe-Coburg from 1722.

Luise was sixteen years old when she married Duke Ernst I of Saxe-Coburg in July 1817 at Friedenstein. He was the eldest son of Duchess Augusta, who recorded the Battle of Saalfeld in her diary. It was a good match for Ernst because Luise was the only child of the reigning duke of Saxe-Gotha and second in line (after her uncle, who was in his forties and unmarried) to inherit the duchy. She brought a substantial dowry to the marriage (which helped to solve Ernst's financial problems), and her inheritance would arise only a few years later in 1825. She also fulfilled her dynastic duty by quickly producing two sons while she was still a teenager—Ernst Junior in 1818 and Albert in 1819.

But the marriage was unhappy almost from the start. There was a big age gap between the couple; at thirty-three, Ernst was more than twice his wife's age when they married. Also he was a longtime womaniser who had scandals in his past, which had already scuppered a much grander royal engagement to the tsar of Russia's sister.[111] In her memoirs published in 1823, one of his ex-lovers accused Ernst of seducing her when she was fifteen and then abandoning her and their child.[112] Courtiers made sure they passed on the stories of her husband's infidelities to Luise, and soon she was complaining of loneliness and telling Ernst that 'pleasuring' himself with someone else could not make him happy because it was a sin.[113]

Ernst saw no reason to change his ways. Aristocratic men like him were not expected to be faithful; besides he had married Luise for her money and not for love. Luise was a nice girl and she seems to have started off with the best intentions. When Ernst brought her home after the wedding her mother-in-law, Augusta, wrote in her diary

> She is a dear, sweet little person, not exactly pretty, but very attractive in her extreme youth and vivacity. She has expressive large blue eyes and a pleasant voice. She speaks well with much good sense and is most amiable, so that one must like her.[114]

But Luise was young, romantic, lonely, and badly treated by her husband. She began to enjoy flirtations with other men and there were rumours that she was unfaithful. We can't know for sure if the rumours were true, but it's possible that she did have an affair; she certainly began to live openly with one of her suspected lovers, Maximilian von Hanstein, soon after her separation from Ernst. What was sauce for the gander was definitely not sauce for the goose, and Ernst could not tolerate his wife's infidelity. His mother had also changed her tune, and now referred to Luise as 'she who has become a shameless little sinner and marriage breaker.'[115]

In 1824 Ernst and Luise separated, and she was sent to live 250 miles away in St Wendel, in the small principality of Lichtenberg in the Saarland (near the French border). This had been awarded to Ernst at the Congress of Vienna.

The terms of the separation were harsh; Luise was not permitted to see her sons and was given only an allowance whilst Ernst kept control of her fortune. He also wanted to get his hands on her inheritance from the duchy of Saxe-Gotha, so he waited until after her uncle (the last duke) died in 1825 before starting divorce proceedings. In the reshuffle of lands that followed Ernst was awarded Gotha in exchange for Saalfeld, and thereafter the duchy became Saxe-Coburg-Gotha.

So Prince Albert's mother disappeared overnight when he was five and he never saw her again. The trauma of this forced separation must have had an effect on him. He grew up undemonstrative and re-

40. Prince Albert was the second son of Duchess Luise.

served, and with a horror of sexual immorality. Both his father and his brother were libertines, but Albert was different. He never looked at any woman other than his wife and was completely faithful to Queen Victoria. His disapproval of sexual laxity was one of the reasons why he was disliked by the English aristocracy, who considered him a prig and a prude.

After her divorce Luise married Maximilian von Hanstein. It was a happy marriage but the couple did not have many years together; Luise died in 1831 from cancer of the womb. One of the two portraits at Friedenstein is of Luise just before her engagement to Ernst. It shows a girl blossoming into womanhood who gazes serenely over her shoulder with her arms full of roses. The other is of her as a much younger child in a pink dress, hardly more than a toddler, and she is playing with her toys. I like to think that these years at Friedenstein, before she married Ernst, were among the happiest of her life.

Reinhardsbrunn

A brief comment in a guidebook was what sent us to the small town of Friedrichroda in the beautiful Thuringian forest, just a few miles from Gotha. It said that Queen Victoria had come there in 1840 to meet her fiancé, Prince Albert.[116] I have read a lot about Victoria but had never heard this story before, so we decided to visit the schloss and check it out. Although the comment wasn't quite accurate, Victoria did visit Schloss Reinhardsbrunn at Friedrichroda when it was in its heyday, as did many other European royals. Today however it lies stripped out, empty and decaying, and is the subject of a major dispute between the owners and the state of Thuringia.

As we could not find the schloss we called at the tourist information office, to ask for directions and about opening hours, where we were told about the current state of affairs. Since the fall of the Iron Curtain, Reinhardsbrunn has passed through the hands of a series of investors but has so far failed to find an owner willing to make the large investment needed to restore it. It was last sold around 2010, reportedly to a Russian investor for the nominal figure of one euro. The state of Thuringia is trying to buy it back, or expropriate it from the owners, but the problem is that compensation will be based on market value. Also the schloss has been mortgaged, and the mortgages would have to be redeemed. In the meantime it is slowly mouldering away and is the constant target of thieves. The latest theft, of the bells from the belfry, took place only a month or two before we were there.

It was a lucky chance that our visit happened to fall on a day when there was a guided tour of the grounds of Reinhardsbrunn. It is not possible to see inside the schloss, which is shuttered and barred, but on three afternoons a week between April and October there is a tour of the gardens. If we cared to wait for a few hours, we were told in the tourist information office, we would be able to join this. We did care to, and we spent the time exploring the little town, which has a picture-postcard High Street framed by the magnificent backdrop of the forested Thuringian hills.

41. Schloss Reinhardsbrunn was built by Duke Ernst I of Saxe-Coburg in fashionable Gothic Revival style.

Just before the appointed time for our tour of Reinhardsbrunn, we parked the car on a patch of dirt outside some locked iron gates and joined a group of fifteen or sixteen others. The schloss is not visible from the road but as we walked down the drive, past the cavalier house and the stables, it came into sight. Built in Gothic Revival style with towers, turrets, and curved arches, and surrounded by lush but very overgrown gardens, it looked like the palace in *Sleeping Beauty* while still in the middle of its hundred years asleep.

We had a fascinating hour walking the grounds with our knowledgeable guide, who told us its history and showed us pictures of how it all used to look. The tour was in German and our guide did not speak English, but here we were lucky yet again. A young man called Sasha, who was there for an afternoon out with his sister and aunt, stepped in and acted as translator. This kind family invited us home for tea afterwards, where we shared reminiscences about what life had been like on opposite sides of the Iron Curtain.

Duke Ernst I of Saxe-Coburg built Schloss Reinhardsbrunn after his divorce from Luise. Until 1825 Friedrichroda was part of the old duchy of Saxe-Gotha, but after the last duke (Luise's uncle) died, his lands were split and this part came to Ernst I. Starting in the late 1820s he built Reinhardsbrunn on the site of an old monastery that dated back to the eleventh century. Parts of the monastery ruins are incorporated into the schloss buildings; for example, the walls of the stables.

The Saxe-Coburgs were an extraordinary family who rose from obscurity to occupy several European thrones within a couple of generations. When Ernst I succeeded his father as duke in 1806, the family fortunes were at their lowest ebb. Their duchy had been invaded by Napoleon and the revenues sequestered. But by the time Ernst died forty years later, in 1844, his brother was the king of Belgium, his son was married to the queen of England, and his nephew was king-consort of Portugal. More thrones would follow in the future. The family were generally good looking, and their rise in the world began with the marriages made by Ernst and his siblings. Behind these was the guiding hand of their mother, the formidable Duchess Augusta (see Saalfeld). One of her four daughters married the brother of the tsar of Russia, and another the brother of the king of England. As well as Ernst, his two brothers also made advantageous marriages. One married the heiress to the British throne and the other a fabulously rich Hungarian countess. The marriage strategy of the Saxe-Coburgs was so successful that Bismarck would later say that 'Coburg is the stud farm of Europe.'

Because of Ernst's connections, much of Europe's royal circle visited Reinhardsbrunn. It was very easy to check up on Queen Victoria's visits and discover that she went to stay there twice. The first time was in 1842, when she came just for one night with her husband, Albert; the second was twenty years later, in 1862, when she came as a widow and stayed for a month. Victoria was a talented diarist and kept a journal from age thirteen until shortly before her death. The journal is kept in the Royal Archives at Windsor, but a special project during Queen Elisabeth II's diamond jubilee year (2012) was to make it available online. So I went to www.queenvictoriasjournals.org and searched under *Reinhardsbrunn* to find the visits and read what Victoria had written about them.

42. In its heyday, Reinhardsbrunn played host to much of Europe's royal circle.

She arrived at Reinhardsbrunn by train on Friday, 5 September 1862, alighting at the small station at nearby Mechterstädt, where her own carriage and horses (which had come out from England ahead of her) were waiting to drive her the last few miles to the schloss. Victoria was travelling with a large retinue and Ernst II (Albert's brother) and his wife, Alexandrine, were forced to vacate the schloss and stay elsewhere. As well as six of Victoria's nine children and also her half-sister, there were ladies in waiting, gentlemen equerries, the queen's doctor, governesses, and other members of her household, and of course servants.

Victoria was a relatively new widow, Albert having died nine months before, on 14 December 1861. She had been passionately in love with her husband and was still in the full force of a terrible grief that would hardly abate over the rest of her long life (she died in 1901). In twenty-one years of marriage, she had come to rely on Albert totally and was not used to doing anything on her own or to taking any decisions without him. She felt incapable of resuming her ordinary life, of carrying out her duties, or of appearing in public. She wrote in her journal about how difficult it was for her to just step out of the train and into her carriage when she arrived at the station. 'It was terrible for me to feel that I was in Germany <u>alone</u>, without my beloved one.'[117]

She was forty-three years old and, as the reigning queen of a major European country, was still a desirable catch. But Victoria would never marry again. She wore widow's weeds for the rest of her days and devoted herself to keeping Albert's memory alive. This was one of the reasons that Victoria had come abroad. Albert had been planning the marriage of their eldest son when he died, and she wanted to bring his plans to fruition.

I am also anxious to repeat one thing, and that one is my firm resolve, my irrevocable decision, viz. that his wishes—his plans—about everything, his views about everything are to be my law! And no human power will make me swerve from what he decided and wished.[118]

There was general jubilation when Albert Edward, Prince of Wales (always known as Bertie) was born in November 1841. But poor Bertie was a worry to his parents from the start and could never live up to their expectations. He grew up in the shadow of his father's phobia of sexual immorality. Bertie's parents were desperate that he should take after his straightlaced and hardworking father and not after Victoria's Hanoverian family (particularly her licentious uncles), or indeed Albert's own father.

In the summer of 1861 Bertie was in Ireland taking a course with the Grenadier Guards. On his last night, after a wild party, some fellow officers smuggled an actress into his bed. Bertie enjoyed the surprise and the actress, Nellie Clifden, followed him back to London. Inevitably the story leaked out and became the talk of the London clubs. At the time most people might have regarded it as par for the course for an aristocratic young man, but when Albert found out he was devastated. His worst fears for his son were coming true. From that time his illness took a sharp turn for the worse, and within a month he was dead. This was the reason why Victoria always blamed her eldest son for his father's death.

The bride that Albert had been considering for Bertie was Princess Alexandra, the eldest daughter of Prince Christian of Glücksburg, who would become King Christian IX of Denmark (see Glücksburg). He had really wanted a German princess but they were in short supply, and besides Alexandra (known as Alix) was reported to be beautiful, which it was hoped might help to keep Bertie on the straight and narrow. After Albert's death, Victoria determined that Alix's parents must be told about 'poor, wretched Bertie's miserable escapade'[119] but also reassured, in case they thought about calling things off, that she 'looked to his wife as being his salvation.'[120] In reality the Glücksburgs, who were not at all well off, were never going to walk away from this chance of a great marriage for their daughter.

Victoria insisted on vetting Alix, 'so that I could judge, before it is too late, whether she will suit me.'[121] So a meeting was arranged with the princess and her parents at the royal palace at Laeken in Belgium, while Victoria was on route to Reinhardsbrunn. She was delighted with the princess and wrote in her journal for 3 September 1862 that

Alexandra is lovely, such a beautiful refined profile, and quiet ladylike manner, which made such a favourable impression.

Bertie was given the go-ahead, and a few days later he proposed and was accepted. It was only the second time that he and Alix had met. Courtship, or time for the couple to get to know each other, was not considered necessary for royal engagements. The news was telegraphed to his mother at Reinhardsbrunn.

43. Queen Victoria was a new widow when she stayed at Reinhardsbrunn in 1862.

In her journal Victoria sets down the day-to-day activities of her visit to Reinhardsbrunn. She also records a family drama when another of her sons, who was a haemophiliac, had an attack of bleeding while they were there. Haemophilia is a disorder of the blood whereby the component that makes it clot is missing, so any cut or small injury is dangerous as the sufferer could bleed to death. Victoria was a carrier of the disease and her youngest son Leopold a sufferer. Two of her daughters were in turn carriers and through their marriages would take the dreadful disease into other European royal families, where it would bring tragedy and contribute to the collapse of thrones.

Victoria's journal for Saturday, 27 September 1862, written at Reinhardsbrunn, says that nine-year-old Leopold has stuck a pen in the roof of his mouth by accident, causing severe bleeding that cannot be stopped. Over the following days the crisis unfolds as he is unable to eat or sleep, and the bleeding stops and then starts again. A telegraph is sent to Berlin for a second doctor who arrives on 1 October, applies some 'strong stuff' to the boy's mouth, and orders constant pressure with the fingers. The two doctors take turns sitting up all night with their patient, and by morning the bleeding has stopped and the crisis point has been passed. Leopold will even be well enough to go with the rest of the party when they leave the schloss at the end of their visit on Friday, 3 October. It hardly bears thinking about what the poor little boy must have gone through during these days of pain, sickness, and bleeding. Unlike most haemophiliacs, Leopold would live to grow up. He died from a brain haemorrhage following a minor fall when he was thirty.

After World War I, the duchy of Saxe-Coburg was split into two when Coburg voted to become part of the state of Bavaria, leaving the rest of the duchy in Thuringia. This would have profound consequences after World War II, when Thuringia (but not Bavaria) fell behind the Iron Curtain. The family lost Reinhardsbrunn in 1945 when it was expropriated by the Soviets. In the Cold War years the schloss was used as a training centre for policemen and firefighters and later as a state-owned hotel. The hotel eventually closed in 2001, and since then the schloss has been empty and slowly rotting away. But public interest in its fate is growing; there was a television documentary shortly before we were there, and the state of Thuringia is now involved. I hope that when I next visit Reinhardsbrunn, perhaps in a few years' time, I will find that it has been saved and restored and is back in use again.

Residenzschloss, Weimar

Weimar was once the centre of the small duchy of Saxe-Weimar-Eisenach (Saxe-Weimar for short). Its rise in fortunes began in 1552, when Johann Friedrich I moved to Weimar and founded the new duchy. He needed a new residence as he had just been forced to hand over the much bigger and more important electorate of Saxony to his cousin Maurice (see Schloss Saalfeld for this story). But the reason why visitors from all over the world still come to see and enjoy Weimar is that, in 1775, a descendant of Johann Friedrich I invited a budding young writer called Johann Wolfgang von Goethe to come and live there. Today Weimar is a living museum, as a large part of the town has been classified as a UNESCO world heritage site.

The year 1775 was very important in the life of Duke Karl August of Saxe-Weimar. He had succeeded his father as a baby, and during his minority the duchy was governed by his mother, Duchess Anna Amalia. In 1775 Karl August reached his eighteenth birthday and took over the reins of government. He also got married to Princess Luise Auguste of Hesse-Darmstadt. And of lasting importance to Weimar is that he asked the twenty-six-year-old Goethe, whom he had met in Frankfurt the year before, to move to his duchy. The two men became great friends, which was unusual at the time because they came from different social classes. Goethe would live and work in Weimar for more than fifty years, providing the flame that attracted other intellectuals there, including Friedrich Schiller. Goethe and Schiller are the two giants of German literature. My guidebook claimed that the statue of the two outside the German National Theatre in Weimar, where they stand side by side, is the most famous statue in Germany.[122]

When Goethe arrived in Weimar in 1775, it was a complete backwater. The town was nothing more than a few hundred houses clustered around the blackened shell of the old Wilhelmsburg schloss that had burned down the year before. And to reach the town travellers had to negotiate a road in such poor condition that they often preferred to drive their carriages over the fields rather than risk it.[123] The attraction for Goethe was presumably his growing friendship with the duke, and perhaps the opportunity to play an important role in the small duchy. He would become the duke's adviser, a minister of state, and hold many other important roles, including director of the theatre. He would also oversee the building of the new Residenzschloss. During the long reign of Duke Karl August the small duchy of Saxe-Weimar was transformed, with Goethe's help, into the acknowledged intellectual capital of Europe. The period until the two friends died (Karl August in 1828 and Goethe in 1832) is known as Weimar Classicism.[124]

44. Goethe and Schiller lived in Weimar during its golden age; the statue of the two men outside the theatre is said to be the most famous in Germany.

A legacy of this brilliant period is that there is so much for the visitor to see in Weimar. As well as the homes of Goethe, Schiller, and other famous residents, there are archives and museums, the Anna Amalia library, the landscaped Park an der Ilm, the royal crypt, and numerous schlösser. We enjoyed just wandering around the streets of the old town, where history is evident everywhere.

After the old schloss was destroyed by fire, the Saxe-Weimar ducal family were forced to live elsewhere in Weimar until it was rebuilt. The new duke moved into the Fürstenhaus, his younger brother into Schloss Tiefurt, and their mother into the Wittumspalais (Widow's Palace), all of which are still there today. In the Wittumspalais visitors can still see the room and the table where Duchess Anna Amalia held her weekly 'round-table' evenings with Goethe, Schiller, and other intellectuals.

Duchess Anna Amalia is another important figure in the history of the duchy. Born a princess of Brunswick-Wolfenbüttel (which we will visit in the next chapter), she married the duke of Saxe-Weimar in 1756 when she was sixteen. Little more than two years later her young husband was dead of TB (tuberculosis), leaving Anna Amalia with a nine-month-old baby son and another baby on the way. Their second son was born three months after his father's death. Anna Amalia became regent for her infant son and was one of the few women to govern a state in the Holy Roman Empire. She was an intelligent woman with a mind of her own and proved to be a competent ruler. She was very interested in literature and the arts, and it was Anna Amalia who first set up the theatre in Weimar and also saved the great library (which now bears her name) from the fire of 1774 because she had it moved into the Grünes Schloss (Green Palace) as a building of its own.

There is a very interesting picture of the old Wilhelmsburg schloss on fire by an unknown artist, showing flames billowing from the roof and crowds of figures trying to save the contents. Most of it was destroyed; only the tower and a group of buildings on the south side, called the Bastille Ensemble, survived. Karl August set up a committee under the chairmanship of Goethe to oversee the rebuilding, but progress was slow and money short. The Napoleonic Wars caused further delay and it was not until 1803, after nearly thirty years, that the ducal family were able to move back in. The new Residenzschloss was very different in style to the baroque Wilhelmsburg that it replaced. It was built in the new neoclassical style that was popular at the beginning of the nineteenth century. The contrast is still very noticeable today between the baroque tower and the grey-and-yellow Bastille with the cool cream neoclassical schloss next to it.

45. The neoclassical Residenzschloss at Weimar (right) is a great contrast in style to the old baroque schloss it replaced (left).

The schloss museum includes the main rooms used by the family and we concentrated our visit on these. I loved the elegant ballroom, but my favourite rooms were the two showing family portraits. The first has a beautiful series of portraits of Karl August, his wife Luise, and their three children, painted in the 1790s by Johann Friedrich August Tischbein. These are the earliest family portraits on show that were painted from life, as everything in the ducal collection before 1774 was destroyed in the fire. In the other room with its fascinating gallery of the duchesses of Saxe-Weimar, many of the portraits date from long after their subjects were dead. They include a delightful portrait of Sibylle of Cleves, who was the wife of the founder of the duchy, Johann Friedrich I. With her long red hair flowing in waves over her shoulders and a coronet of flowers, she looks almost Pre-Raphaelite. Sibylle was the sister of Anne of Cleves who, for a short time, was the fourth wife of Henry VIII of England. Anne was queen of England for only six months and was smart enough to agree to a quick divorce when she did not please her husband.

Also in the gallery of duchesses is a portrait, painted from life in 1854, of the most famous bride to come to Saxe-Weimar. This was Grand Duchess Maria Paulowna of Russia, who married Duke Karl Friedrich, the eldest son of Karl August. She was immensely rich and one room in the schloss is devoted to her dowry. We will find out more about her at our next schloss.

The Residenzschloss was at the top of my list of things to visit in Weimar, but it was a shock when we got there and my passport was demanded as security for the audio guide. This was completely out of proportion, as there was nothing special about the audio guide at all—indeed large parts of the German commentary were missing from the English version. Perhaps it was just residual bureaucracy left over from the old East German days. There is much to interest lovers of royal history at the Residenzschloss, including an amazing genealogical chart of the family that stretches down the stairwell. This covers more than five hundred years, from the split of the Wettin into two branches to the death of the last duke of Saxe-Weimar, and it shows how all the small Ernestine duchies were descended from the unfortunate Johann Friedrich I. But compared to some other museums the contents were not best displayed; there is no English guidebook; and the attendants, at least while we were there, seemed completely uninterested in the visitors. Fortunately our next schloss would provide a better experience.

Belvedere

From the Goethe House in the centre of Weimar a long, straight road leads out of the town to the southeast. It runs alongside the Ilm River and past the landscaped parks of the Residenzschloss (Park an der Ilm) and Schloss Tiefurt until, after three kilometres, it reaches Schloss Belvedere. It was Maria Paulowna who had the idea to create this 'green alley' joining up the three schlösser.[125] It seemed like a long three kilometres; there were few signs to the schloss, and several times we thought we must have lost our way. But suddenly we turned a corner and there was the car park and a map of the gardens—we had arrived at Schloss Belvedere.

As we walked from the car park, the whole tenor of the day changed. A grey, rainy morning in Weimar had become a sunny spring afternoon in the country, with blue skies and singing birds. The path led past the music school in the schloss gardens, and the music drifting from the open windows was in keeping with our uplifted mood. And when the path emerged into the open space in front of the schloss, it was such a special moment that it made me draw in my breath and gasp. Belvedere is a jewel of a schloss and it was my favourite in Thuringia.

The schloss is set in a perfect location, surrounded by its large gardens and with the most glorious views across the Thuringian countryside to Weimar in the distance. It was Duke Ernst August I who found this place on a hunting trip and built the schloss in the 1730s. He based it on the summer residence of Prince Eugene of Savoy in Vienna, which he had seen and admired. Prince Eugene's palace is called Belvedere, so that is how our schloss got its name. Ernst August I was the father-in-law of Anna Amalia. He was forty-nine years old and had already lost four sons as children when his heir, Ernst August II, was finally born in 1738. Ernst August II also died young, of TB when he was nineteen, but he had already lived long enough to succeed his father, marry Anna Amalia, and father two sons of his own. His story helped me to better understand why all these princes and princesses were married so young, almost as soon as they reached puberty. It was because killer diseases such as smallpox and TB, not to mention death in childbirth, were no respecter of rank, wealth, or age. Life might be short, but the family line must go on.

Schloss Belvedere is most associated with Grand Duchess Maria Paulowna who was the wife of Duke Karl Friedrich. After they married, the groom's father, Karl August, gave the schloss to the young couple as a summer residence. Maria Paulowna was the third of six daughters of Tsar Paul of Russia. They were the trophy brides of their day and highly coveted on the royal marriage market, so it may seem a surprise that in 1804 she married only the heir to a minor German duchy. But there were longstanding links between the Saxe-Weimar and Russian royal families, as Paul's first wife had been a sister of the wife of Karl August, Duchess Luise (for the death of Paul's first wife please see Schloss Eutin).[126] In addition, although the duchy was small, Karl August and his cultured court were much admired across Europe. As an enlightened ruler he was the model for the young Prince Albert, later prince consort of Great Britain, growing up in neighbouring Saxe-Coburg.[127]

46. Belvedere is a jewel that fits perfectly into its sylvan surroundings.

Schloss Belvedere is not huge or monumental; instead it is what I call a little schloss, or *schlösschen*. The main schloss building has a beautifully proportioned and elegant front elevation painted in soft and muted colours—pale apricot, dusty pink, and white. This is topped by a lantern tower with an open gallery around it, to better enjoy the marvellous views. To either side of the main building, but attached to it only at the first-floor level, are two much smaller pavilions with pointed domes, each having just a single room per floor. In front of the schloss is a circular lawn with a fountain in the middle, and on either side of this are the two cavalier houses and other supplementary buildings. Everything is harmonious and on the right scale here; the schloss seems to fit quite perfectly into its sylvan surroundings. In this way it reminds me of Pavlovsk, the perfect palace outside St Petersburg where Maria Paulowna was brought up. Perhaps this is one reason why she loved Schloss Belvedere. Maria Paulowna was a keen gardener, and she and her husband completely redesigned the schloss gardens into a romantic landscaped park which survives to this day. It includes the Russian garden created in 1811 to one side of the schloss, which is a replica of the Russian royal family's private garden at Pavlovsk. After her husband died Belvedere was the widow's residence for Maria Paulowna, and she died there in 1859.

The marriage of Karl Friedrich and Maria Paulowna was arranged by their families as early as 1799 when the bride-to-be was only thirteen, although the wedding ceremony itself did not take place until 1804. It was a major coup for Saxe-Weimar as the bride would bring not only an enormous dowry, but also close links with Russia which, it was hoped, would help protect the duchy against Napoleon. The delay before the wedding enabled the rebuilding of the Residenzschloss in Weimar to be completed so that the new bride would have a home fit for her high station.

Maria Paulowna arrived in Weimar accompanied by a baggage train of eighty carts stacked with crates of fabulous Russian treasures. When this lavish dowry was put on public show, such a display of wealth stunned the local populace.[128] As well as her trousseau and expensive jewellery, there was linen, silverware, porcelain, chandeliers, and furniture. The centrepiece was a magnificent four-poster bed crowned with the Russian eagle, which is still on display in the Residenzschloss. Under the marriage contract it was agreed that Maria Paulowna could keep her Russian Orthodox faith, so also in those crates were religious icons and furnishings for her personal chapel.

If Weimar had a golden age when Goethe lived there during the reign of Karl August, it also enjoyed a second silver age under Karl Friedrich and his wife.[129] Maria Paulowna was a cultured woman who continued to encourage artists and scholars to Weimar. One of these was the celebrated pianist and composer Franz Liszt, who was appointed *kapellmeister* (or musical director) to the court and lived in Weimar for over thirty years. His legacy today is the Franz Liszt Music Conservatoire, which was founded in 1872 and is housed in a cavalier house at Schloss Belvedere.

Chart 13 is a family tree for the dukes and grand dukes of Saxe-Weimar (it was raised to a grand duchy by the Congress of Vienna). Through Maria Paulowna the small duchy was connected to the great courts of Europe, and her children married well. Her only surviving son, Karl Alexander, made another great marriage for Saxe-Weimar to Princess Sophie, the only daughter of the king of the Netherlands. The bride and groom were first cousins as Sophie's mother was Maria Paulowna's sister. And Maria Paulowna's second daughter, Augusta, married Prince Wilhelm, later king of Prussia and German kaiser.

The exterior of Schloss Belvedere was so beautiful, like an exquisite piece of porcelain, that we almost feared to go inside lest it might spoil the mood. But we need not have worried as it was a very pleasant experience. We received a friendly welcome from the attendants; there were guidebooks in English for the schloss and the gardens and a fully functional audio guide; and there was no requirement to leave my passport as security. And best of all, instead of felt overshoes the schloss had carpet runners on the floors with a polite notice for visitors to please walk on these. At one point a large and rather scary-looking attendant walked quickly up to my husband and began speaking to him in German. We were apprehensive that perhaps we had inadvertently done something wrong. But it turned out that my husband had dust on the back of his coat, and the attendant was advising him to brush it off!

The interior of Belvedere has a light summery feel and, of course, magnificent views from the main rooms on the first floor. The schloss houses a collection of porcelain, glass, and furniture, and there are also family portraits. We were the only visitors and had a lovely afternoon.

The Spargel Season

If you visit Germany in the spring, as we did, then you are bound to run slap bang into the spargel season. Spargel is asparagus, but it's a very different type from the green variety we are familiar with in the UK. Spargel is blanched white during cultivation by earthing up the soil around the growing shoots to exclude daylight. It looks and tastes very different to green asparagus.

During the three months of the season (from April to June), spargel is ubiquitous in Germany. Germans love to eat it and call it weiss gold (white gold) or königsgemuse (the king's vegetable). To supply the demand, booths spring up by the side of what seems every road selling spargel by the kilo, together with the other fresh crop in season—strawberries. And every eating place, from fine dining restaurants to informal country inns, will have a special spargel menu. It's only ever eaten during the season; you will never ever find spargel (unlike green asparagus in the UK) imported from the other side of the world and on sale in supermarkets all year round.

The classic way of eating spargel is simple but delicious—just accompanied by boiled potatoes and either hollandaise sauce or melted butter (always hollandaise for me). If you like you can add to this from a menu of choices—perhaps a piece of steak, or Wiener schnitzel or salmon. My personal favourite is spargel mit schinken (cooked as opposed to cured ham). So if you are in Germany during the spargel season, I would urge you to give this wonderful vegetable a try.

Heidecksburg

Prince Luis Ferdinand of Prussia spent the last night of his life at Schloss Heidecksburg in Rudolstadt. The prince was in command of the vanguard of the Prussian army, and the schloss was his headquarters. He was an impetuous young man and was keen to get at the advancing French army and cover his name with glory. By all accounts he was the life and soul of a hilarious party at the schloss that evening.[130] The following day (10 October 1806), he was killed at the Battle of Saalfeld (for the death of Luis Ferdinand see Schloss Saalfeld).

Heidecksburg was the residence of the princes of an independent state called Schwarzburg-Rudolstadt. This was another of the principalities and duchies that once made up what is today the federal state of Thuringia. Schwarzburg-Rudolstadt was very small—in 1905 it had an area of less than a thousand square kilometres and a population of less than a hundred thousand.[131] Nevertheless it survived right up until the end of the German monarchy, coming through both the savage cut in the number of territories at the beginning of the nineteenth century (in the process called mediatisation) and Bismarck's wars and annexations of the 1860s. In fact when Prince Günther Viktor of Schwarzburg-Rudolstadt abdicated on 23 November 1918, he was the last of all the rulers of the German sovereign states to go.

During our schloss tours my husband and I visit a lot of different schlösser in a relatively short space of time. To keep them separate and fix each one in my mind, I try to come up with a word or short phrase that encapsulates it. So using this system, Reinhardsbrunn (which once hosted European royalty but now lies abandoned and neglected) is 'the ghost schloss'; Saalfeld is the schloss where we got the 'best welcome'; and exquisite Belvedere is simply 'the jewel'. From the moment that I stepped inside Heidecksburg, there was no doubt in my mind about the right tag for this one. Because of its series of elaborately decorated rococo rooms, where make-believe figures gambol through an imaginary landscape, this is 'the fantasy schloss'. I came away wondering how on earth the ruling family of such a small state managed to acquire the wealth to create all this.

In 1735 fire swept through the schloss at Heidecksburg, destroying much of the north and west wings. The reigning prince at the time, Friedrich Anton (1692–1744), decided to rebuild but his plans did not go smoothly at first. His first choice of architect died and the second moved at too slow a pace for the prince's liking. So in 1741 he set up a commission under the leadership of his son, hereditary prince Johann Friedrich (1721–1767), to oversee the work. Johann Friedrich made a good choice when he appointed yet a third architect. This was Gottfried Heinrich Krohne, who was the court architect for Saxe-Weimar and had already worked on the building of Schloss Belvedere.

Krohne retained much of his predecessor's plans but did make some important changes. One of these was to alter the interior decoration

47. Schloss Heidecksburg where, in the decoration of the rococo rooms, make-believe figures gambol through an imaginary landscape.

of the west wing, which houses the staterooms. Instead of the simple decoration originally intended, Krohne decided to use the newly fashionable rococo style. We would see rooms at the schloss in later styles, such as early nineteenth-century neoclassicism and late nineteenth-century historicism, but it was the rococo reception rooms in the west wing that made the biggest impact on us.

The Principality of Schwarzburg-Rudolstadt

The principality dates from a division of the Schwarzburg family lands between two brothers in 1599. The family itself was more ancient, going back to the eleventh century, and there had been divisions and amalgamations of their lands before. But the division of 1599 into Schwarzburg-Rudolstadt and Schwarzburg-Sonderhausen would prove a lasting one; the two would not be reunited until 1909.

Schwarzburg-Rudolstadt was originally a county ruled by a count (graf). In 1711 the little territory was raised to a principality of the Holy Roman Empire. After this there would be ten ruling princes before the monarchy came to an end, starting with Ludwig Friedrich (1667–1718) and ending with Günther Viktor (1852–1925).

The interior of Heidecksburg can be visited only by guided tour and these are in German. The schloss is not very accessible to a foreign visitor as there is no guidebook or audio guide in English. I was lent an English handout to take with me on the guided tour but found this disappointing because although helpful on the décor, it had no information at all about the Schwarzburg-Rudolstadt family. I am sorry to say that I also became frustrated with our tour guide. There were only six of us on the tour and, as I knew that our guide spoke a little English, I was hopeful that we might be able to pick up some information. But it soon became clear that this was not going to happen. Our guide was on a timetable and spoke German too quickly for my husband to understand. She also seemed to resolutely avoid catching my eye when

I wanted to ask a question. Perhaps she was nervous about practicing her English. So we gave up and decided just to enjoy the experience of wandering through these amazing rooms.

The suite of staterooms built by Prince Johann Friedrich is centred on the Festival Hall, or ballroom. This is flanked on either side by matching anterooms—the Red Hall and Red Corner Chamber on one side and the Green Hall and Green Corner Chamber on the other. Running behind all the rooms and connecting them on the courtyard side is the Marble Gallery. These rooms are decorated in the new rococo style, which had recently arrived in Germany from France when the prince appointed Krohne as his architect. The style is characterised by elaborate and exuberant decoration and the use of curves and countercurves. Pastel colours, gold, mirrors, and glass help to create a feeling of elegance and lightness, and naturalistic paintings add to the mood of playfulness and informality. In the paintings at Heidecksburg beautiful people frolic and gambol in an idyllic natural landscape. They are not real people or real landscape views; the paintings are part of the rococo decoration. In the Marble Gallery there are twelve of these fantasy landscapes showing imaginary people from all around the world.

The high point of the reception rooms is the Festival Hall, which is two floors or twelve metres tall. I don't think I have ever been in a room that more assaults the senses (in a nice way). It glitters and glistens with crystal chandeliers, china, mirrors, and little pieces of marble embedded in the stuccoed walls. The colours are light and harmonious—ivory and gold, pink, yellow and grey. Everywhere there are curves and flourishes, with decorative plasterwork enhanced by golden gilding. A golden balcony runs at the second-story level down one side of the room, supported by four bare-chested figures with their muscles rippling. In the painting on the ceiling the Olympian gods are listening to the singing of Apollo. More fantasy paintings adorn the walls. There are just no straight lines in this room—even the walls curve and wave in and out. The shell is the symbol of rococo and in the corners of the hall, which are rounded off, are shell-shaped niches or buffets to display china and other precious ornaments. This room was always meant for music and has good acoustics. The guide played us a tape of music by Philipp Heinrich Erlebach, who was kapellmeister at Heidecksburg for thirty-three years.

The magnificence of the schloss interiors made me want to find out more about the family that created them. I asked about the history of the Schwarzburg-Rudolstadt family in the shop at Heidecksburg, but the only thing they could suggest was that I buy a book in German because it contained a pullout genealogical chart.[132] This did indeed prove very helpful and showed me that the family were poor dynastic breeders who eventually ran out of sons. There seems to be very little written in English about this royal house. The only thing I could find was an article by Charlotte Zeepvat in her excellent series on Europe's royal families in the *Royalty Digest Quarterly* journal.

When Georg Albert (who was the ninth of the ten reigning princes) died unmarried in 1890, the succession had to go back two generations and then down again to find the next prince (see chart 14). He was succeeded by his second cousin Günther Viktor, who was the grandson of the younger brother of the grandfather of Georg Albert. In the Green Corner Chamber there is a charming portrait of the two grandfathers as boys with their three sisters.[133] All five children look to be under eleven or twelve years old and are happily playing together. The eldest boy (Georg Albert's grandfather) has a book in his hand, while his younger brother (Günther Viktor's grandfather) builds a house out of playing cards. Their eldest sister sits at the keyboard, and the two younger girls are playing with their toys. Unfortunately, as was the case with so many portraits in so many schlösser, there was no label on this picture and I am not able to tell you the name of the artist.

When Günther Viktor became the prince he was thirty-seven years old and unmarried. He was the only son of an only son and the last dynastically eligible male in the Schwarzburg-Rudolstadt family. So unless something was done about this soon, a succession crisis was looming. Günther Viktor did get married in 1891, but there were no children.

The family might have looked for an heir from the other Schwarzburg principality created on the old 1599 split, Schwarzburg-Sondershausen. There was an agreement between the two dating from 1713 that should one line die out, the other would reunite the Schwarzburg lands.[134] But the Schwarzburg-Sondershausen line was also down to the last man standing and when their last prince died childless in 1909, it was Günther Viktor who reunited the two principalities and became the prince of Schwarzburg-Rudolstadt-Sondershausen (or simply the prince of Schwarzburg). The lack of heirs meant that the family was forced to address an old skeleton in the cupboard—the morganatic marriage forty years before of Prince Friedrich Günther. There was a son of this marriage but the question was, should he be eligible to succeed?

Friedrich Günther (who died in 1867) was the seventh reigning prince of Schwarzburg-Rudolstadt, so there were two others between him and Günther Viktor. The relevant genealogy is shown in chart 14. Friedrich Günther had three sons from his first marriage, but they all predeceased their mother, who died in 1854. The sixty-one-year-old prince married again the following year, to twenty-year-old Gräfin (countess) Helena von Raina, and presumably hoped to father another heir. Helena was aristocratic but not royal because her father, who was a prince of Anhalt, had made a morganatic marriage. In an attempt to rectify this and make her of equal birth, she was adopted by her uncle, Prince Wilhelm of Anhalt, a week before her wedding and declared to be a princess.[135] It didn't cut any ice with the Schwarzburg-Rudolstadt family, and a few months later Helena's marriage was declared to be morganatic. She died three days after giving birth to twins (a boy and a girl) in 1860. Her little boy was named Sizzo, after the founder of the house of Schwarzburg, but he wasn't eligible to become the reigning prince because his parents' marriage was not dynastic.

But as the years went by it became increasingly obvious that there was no one else, particularly after the marriage of Günther Viktor proved childless. So eventually, in 1896, the Schwarzburg family house rules were changed and Sizzo was accepted as heir presumptive to both the principalities of Schwarzburg-Rudolstadt and Schwarzburg-Sonderhausen. He married the following year, aged thirty-six, and in due course became the father of an only son. But the monarchy came to an end before Sizzo could succeed, and the breach in the family over his parents' marriage seems never to have been healed.[136]

Falling in Love outside the Royal Circle—Morganatic Marriage

The concept of morganatic marriage was developed to recognise marriages between partners of unequal social status. In most cases the husband was of royal birth and his wife of a lower social standing, although occasionally it was the other way around. The marriage did not confer royal rank on the wife or children of the marriage, and they had limited rights of inheritance. It was sometimes called a 'left-handed marriage' because the bridegroom gave the bride his left hand in the wedding ceremony rather than the right.

The parameters for morganatic marriage were set by each dynastic house, and there was inevitably a degree of flexibility and pragmatism. When Duke Georg Wilhelm of Celle fell in love with a French aristocrat, his family refused to sanction their marriage. The couple did marry, first privately in 1666 (called a marriage of conscience) and then morganatically in 1676. The family eventually recognised the marriage officially in 1680, which cleared the way for the couple's only child to marry her cousin and unite the family wealth and lands. A century later, King Friedrich Wilhelm II of Prussia used the concept in a somewhat cavalier way to sanction his bigamy. While still married to his official dynastic wife (Queen Friederike), he made two more morganatic marriages in succession in the 1780s.

As a concept, morganatic marriage did not apply in the same way in all the royal houses. When Tsar Alexander II married his mistress in 1880, just a month after his wife's death, he made his new wife a princess and legitimised their children. She did not however become tsarina of Russia. When Edward VIII wanted to marry his mistress in 1936, one concern was that there was no clear concept of morganatic marriage in Great Britain, so Mrs Simpson may have automatically become queen.

As we left Heidecksburg the lingering image in my mind was of the amazing Festival Hall. If I had to imagine the perfect ballroom for Cinderella's ball in a film by Disney, this room would be it. When I mentioned this to our tour guide, she was appalled and at pains to assure me that everything was genuine. To her mind 'Disney' was associated with the fake or artificial. These rococo rooms are definitely the real thing but they are also fantastic, and for me Heidecksburg will always be 'the fantasy schloss'. And just to reinforce this, there is an exhibition in the old kitchens called *Rococo in Miniature*. The result of fifty years of work by the creators, this is a miniature eighteenth-century world of make-believe kingdoms and palaces peopled by hundreds of tiny figures.

Schwarzburg

Schloss Schwarzburg is the ancestral seat of the Schwarzburg family. There has been a schloss on this site for as long as the family has been known, which is around a thousand years. Most German castles were well sited but this location simply takes the prize. For defensive purposes it must be well-nigh perfect; for natural beauty it could not be bettered. As I stood and gazed at the schloss, what was running through my mind was ... wow! Wow! WOW! I only hope I can describe the site in a way that does it justice.

The schloss is built on a high mountain ridge in a bend of the Schwarza River. The sides of the ridge are steep and covered in trees, so the schloss buildings on the top seem to rise above a frill of greenery. The ridge is long and narrow and the river runs along one side, loops around the end, and then runs back parallel down the other side. This means the site is surrounded by the river on three sides, and the only access is a narrow piece of land at the open end, where there is a sort of causeway. Because the ridge is narrow the buildings are strung out in a line, one behind the other. First comes the gatehouse and the armoury, then the schloss, the schloss church, the Emperors' Hall (see later), and finally at the end of the ridge, the baroque garden. There are the most stunning views from this garden high above the river valley, out over the green wooded hills which stretch away into the distance all around. There was perfect peace here, with no sound except a waterfall and the birds singing. This is a spectacularly scenic location which has an almost alpine feel. Perhaps this was a reason why Schwarzburg was the schloss that Hitler coveted.

48. The natural beauty of the site of Schloss Schwarzburg is unsurpassed.

After the fall of the German monarchy, Schwarzburg became the property of the new Free State of Thuringia, but the Schwarzburg-Rudolstadt family was granted the right of residence. After Günther Viktor (the last prince) died in 1925 his widow, Anna Luise, continued to use the schloss until her right to live there was summarily terminated by the Nazi government in 1940. They had decided to turn it into a Reich guesthouse (*Reichgästeheim*) for visiting dignitaries. Anna Luise received compensation but had to leave her home at a few days' notice. The project was initially classified as essential to the war effort and work on the conversion began. The schloss was stripped out and gutted, and parts of it were demolished. But as the tide of World War II turned against Germany the plans had to be abandoned, and in 1942 all work ceased. Schwarzburg was left an uninhabitable ruin and that is largely how it still remains.[137]

Over the years there have been various proposals to reconstruct the schloss, to use for different purposes, but mostly these have failed due to the huge cost involved. Only the small building called the Kaisersaal (or Emperors' Hall) was renovated and opened as a museum in 1971. After the reunification of Germany ownership passed in the 1990s to the Thuringian state heritage organisation (Stiftung Thüringer Schlösser und Gärten), and since then plans for renovation of the schloss have gradually moved forward and some funding has been found. We could not get up close to the main schloss building, which is fenced off and boarded up, but could see enough to tell that it is in a terrible state. But there is scaffolding up and a large hoarding announces that a project is underway. We were told that the work involves a reconstruction of the exterior of the schloss only and that the interiors will be modern. It should be completed in 2019, in time for the centenary of the signing of the Weimar constitution. The president of the German republic, Friedrich Ebert, was staying in Schwarzburg, in the local hotel, when he signed this on 11 August 1919.

The renovation of the armoury is more advanced and this is expected to open as a museum in 2017. Before the Nazis took over the schloss, Schwarzburg was famous for its armoury, which was first mentioned as early as the fourteenth century. The armoury building housed a unique collection of weaponry and armour that had been put together by the Schwarzburg-Rudolstadt family over the generations. In 1940 the Nazis had the building cleared, intending to use it as a garage, and since then the collection has been in storage. But both the building and the collection are now under renovation and will be reunited in the new Schwarzburg museum of weapons and armoury.

147

49. Schwarzburg was gutted by the Nazis and left an uninhabitable ruin.

Until that time however, the Kaisersaal is the thing to visit at Schwarzburg. This takes its name from the fascinating picture gallery of portraits of the Holy Roman emperors. This is an unusual gallery because the pictures are not hung on the walls in the usual way, but painted high up on wall panels in a lantern roof. There were originally forty-eight of them, covering all the emperors up to Karl VI, who held the post when the Kaisersaal was built. Some have been lost but many of the portraits are still there, and they include Emperor Günther XXI, who was a Schwarzburg.

The Schwarzburgs were an ancient and distinguished family but, as far as I can find out, never produced anyone who is really famous. No Schwarzburg princesses married kings, and no Schwarzburg princes earned glory by winning great battles. Günther XXI of Schwarzburg-Blankenburg (1324–1349) may be the most famous of the clan, and even he was only the Holy Roman emperor very briefly. His election in early 1349 seems to have been a bit of a muddle and he abdicated a few months later in favour of his rival, Karl IV of Luxembourg.[138] The changeover must have been amicable because when Günther died later in the same year, the new emperor afforded him royal honours.

The Kaisersaal building and its gallery of emperors dates from the second decade of the eighteenth century, when the family were upgrading the schloss in keeping with their rise in rank (in 1711 the grafs of Schwarzburg-Rudolstadt were promoted to imperial princes). The ground floor was used as an orangery (to bring tender plants indoors in the winter), and the upstairs gallery of emperors was for show and entertaining.

Today the building houses a small but quite fascinating museum about the history of Schwarzburg. With so much of the schloss still in ruins, I particularly liked all the prints, pictures, postcards, and photos showing its appearance over the centuries. Also interesting was the display case of memorabilia from the visit of Queen Wilhelmina of the Netherlands in 1900. Wilhelmina had just become engaged to Duke Heinrich of Mecklenburg-Schwerin and was doing the rounds in Germany to get to know his relations. Heinrich was very closely related to the Schwarzburg-Rudolstadt family, as his mother (Marie) was the sister of Günther Viktor. Wilhelmina stayed for a month (8 May–5 June 1900) in the Gasthaus Weisser Hirsch (the White Hart), which is still there today and still in business as a hotel. It is very close to the schloss, at the end of the entrance causeway. Wilhelmina and Heinrich were married in The Hague on 7 February 1901, when Günther Viktor and his wife Anna Luise were among the guests.

It was the museum attendant at the Kaisersaal who got me interested in Anna Luise. This lovely lady welcomed us and was very excited about the opportunity to practice her English. She referred to Anna Luise as the Last Princess (Die Letzte Fürstin) and encouraged me to buy the biography of her, which has the same title.[139] She must be called this because her husband was the last ruling prince to abdicate in 1918. Anna Luise was born in 1871 and died in 1950, and her life spanned an extraordinary period of upheaval in Germany. Born a princess in the German Empire, she died a commoner in East Germany having lived through the end of the monarchy, two World Wars, the Third Reich, and the division of Germany. She was a keen photographer, and at Heidecksburg we saw a dressing room that was converted into a darkroom for her. She left behind hundreds of photographs documenting her life, and some of these are on display in the Kaisersaal.

Anna Luise married Prince Günther Viktor in 1891, when she was twenty years old. Her new husband was nineteen years older and had succeeded to the title the year before. It was an arranged marriage and the Schwarzburg-Rudolstadt family were desperate for an heir, as the house was in grave danger of dying out. Anna Luise obligingly soon became pregnant, but the baby arrived prematurely and was stillborn. She suffered from complications and was unable to have more children. Both childlessness and the death of a child are very hard to bear and for Anna Luise it must have been even worse, given the heavy expectations of her. She became unconventional in the way she dressed, eschewing fashion and cutting her hair short. One quote calls her 'fabulously inelegant in a white blouse.'[140] She and Günther seemed to have had a poor relationship with Prince Sizzo, who from 1896 was heir to the principality. Much later in life, in 1942, Anna Luise adopted her grown-up nephew.

In January 1919, just a few weeks after her husband's abdication, Anna Luise wrote in a letter to a friend that she would try to find a new role that would make her life worth living. She showed fortitude and optimism throughout her life, and this is the reason why her biographer suggests that 'To make life worth living at all times' could be Anna Luise's life motto.[141] She was the only one of the previous royal rulers in that part of Germany who did not leave to go to the West after World War II.

50. The life of Anna Luise spanned a period of extraordinary upheaval.

7

LOWER SAXONY AND THE DUKES OF BRUNSWICK-WOLFENBÜTTEL

So here we are again in Lower Saxony to finish our tour and see the last five schlösser. On this second visit to the state we will find out more about the German national anthem and meet the family of the longterm mistress of George I. But we start with the principality of Brunswick-Wolfenbüttel and the royal family who were famous for their soldiers and their brides.

Braunschweig

Over the centuries the greatest hazard to the survival of schlösser has been fire, and we visited several that had suffered from fire during their history. But Braunschweig must surely hold the record because it has been severely damaged and rebuilt three times! The first time was during the riots of 1830 when the schloss was burned down by arson; the second was when a kitchen fire got out of hand in 1865; and the third was the bombing raids during World War II. The remains of the burnt-out schloss were demolished in 1960, and a public garden was laid out on the site. The decision to rebuild a third time was hugely controversial because of the plan to use the schloss as a shopping centre.

The Dukes of Brunswick-Wolfenbüttel

The House of Brunswick, with the family name of Guelph or Welf, dates back to at least the twelfth century. Like the other ancient houses, there were numerous divisions and reunifications of land over the centuries. In the first half of the seventeenth century, however, there was a lasting split between two brothers, with the elder taking Brunswick-Wolfenbüttel and the younger Brunswick-Lüneburg. As happened in other families, it would be the junior line that outshone the senior; the dukes of Brunswick-Lüneburg went on to become electors of Hannover in 1692 and kings of Great Britain in 1714. The Brunswick-Lüneburg line was included in my first book, Schloss I. *This book features Brunswick-Wolfenbüttel.*

During the Napoleonic Wars Brunswick-Wolfenbüttel was occupied by the French and became part of the new kingdom of Westphalia, set up by Napoleon for his brother. At the end of the wars in 1815, it was reestablished as the independent duchy of Brunswick. Hannover was still held by the Brunswick-Lüneburg line and was also restored, as a kingdom.

The Brunswick-Wolfenbüttel line died out in 1884, with the death of the last duke of Brunswick from this line, William VIII. The duchy of Brunswick should then have passed to the Brunswick-Lüneburg line under an old family agreement. However this was prevented by Prussia because of their intransigence over their Hanoverian rights. King George V of Hannover had been deposed and his country annexed by Prussia after siding with Austria in the 1866 Seven Weeks' War. After a long interregnum it was eventually agreed that Ernst August III, the grandson of George V, should become duke of Brunswick when he married the Prussian princess, Viktoria Luise, in 1913. However, he was not duke for long, abdicating his rights, along with the other ruling German princes, in November 1918.

51. Schloss Braunschweig was destroyed in World War II but rebuilt and opened as a shopping centre in 2007.

The Schloss-Arkaden (Schloss Arcade) was opened in 2007. Only the front and one side have been built as a replica of the old schloss; the rest looks similar to modern retail space anywhere. Our route into the city centre took us round the back of the shopping centre first, so that it was a surprise suddenly to turn the corner and see the schloss. The front is monumental (over two hundred metres long and twenty metres high), and access to the shops is through what would have been the main entrance, with a grand portico topped by a huge statue of a quadriga (a chariot drawn by four horses abreast). Entrance to the museum is by a door in the left wing.

The debate about the most appropriate way of preserving ruined schlösser is not a new one; it has been going on since the Rhine castles were rebuilt in the nineteenth century. The argument is whether the ruins should just be maintained as they are to prevent further decay, or the schloss be reconstructed as accurately to the original as possible. Or is it justifiable to make adaptions or improvements to make the building more suited to the modern day? I can see all sides of the argument, but I do not have a problem with what has been done at Braunschweig. The front of the schloss looks good in the space that was designed for it, and I like the museum. Without the shopping centre to make it commercially viable, it would never have been possible to rebuild.

We arrived first thing in the morning, before the shops or museum were open. It had been raining and the stones of the wide pavement in front of the schloss glistened. On this, to each side of the portico, is

a statue of a man on horseback. These are the two dukes of Brunswick-Wolfenbüttel who died defending their homeland against the French in the Napoleonic Wars: Duke Karl Wilhelm Ferdinand (1735–1806) and his son, Duke Friedrich Wilhelm (1771–1815). Father and son were part of a tradition of Wolfenbüttel princes who were professional soldiers and served in the Prussian army. This began when Prince Ferdinand joined the Prussian army following the famous double marriage of 1733, when his sister Elisabeth Christine married Frederick the Great of Prussia (then crown prince) and his elder brother Karl I married Frederick's younger sister Philippine Charlotte (see chart 15).

52. Karl Wilhelm Ferdinand of Brunswick-Wolfenbüttel was the greatest soldier of his age.

Duke Karl Wilhelm Ferdinand followed in his Uncle Ferdinand's footsteps and also joined the Prussian army, where he rose to the rank of field marshal. He is regarded as the greatest soldier of his age; the story is that when hostilities broke out between revolutionary France and the Holy Roman Empire, he was offered command of the armies of both sides.[142] He stuck with Prussia and in 1792 issued the famous Brunswick Manifesto, declaring that he would invade France to end the revolution and restore the king to power. In fact the tables would be turned, and the duke died on German soil defending his homeland against French invaders. At seventy-one, the duke was still fighting when he was wounded in the eyes at the Battle of Auerstadt in 1806 and died a month later. In her diaries Duchess Augusta of Saxe-Coburg bitterly reproaches Napoleon for hounding the dying duke, who was carried from the battlefield in a litter.[143] Napoleon annexed Brunswick-Wolfenbüttel and it became part of the kingdom of Westphalia.

Friedrich Wilhelm was not as famous as his father. He is known as the Black Duke and remembered mainly for founding the regiment of Brunswick Hussars, who wore black uniforms in mourning for their duchy. Friedrich Wilhelm wears this uniform in his portrait at the schloss. He also died fighting the French at the Battle of Quatre Bras in 1815, two days before the final defeat of Napoleon at Waterloo.

I thought the museum in Schloss Braunschweig was excellent. As well as the permanent exhibition on the history of the schloss, there were two temporary exhibitions. The first of these was called *Following in the Footsteps of Karl I*, and it commemorated the three-hundred-year anniversary of the birth of Duke Karl I. He moved the residence of the duchy from Wolfenbüttel (which we visit next) to the Graue-Hof (or Grey Court) in Braunschweig in 1754. The Grey Court was the original schloss that burned down in 1830. The second exhibition commemorated the one-hundred-year anniversary of the baptism of baby Ernst August (the son of the last duke of Brunswick) in May 1914, and it was an exhibition of royal christening gowns.

Everything in all three exhibitions was extremely well displayed and labelled, and there was lots of interesting looking material to read. My only complaint is that none of this was in English. There was however an English audio guide to the permanent exhibition, and this was the best one of our tour. As well as lively narrative, it offered alternative commentary in each room so that the visitor could choose what to listen to. The curator was kind and helpful, and this was the first time anyone explained their policy on taking photographs and why. I was permitted to take photographs everywhere (but for my own use only) except in the exhibition of christening gowns. This was because all these items had been lent privately to the museum, and they did not own the rights.

The permanent exhibition presents the staterooms as they would have been in the time of Duke Wilhelm, who was the last duke from the Wolfenbüttel line. He was a second son and not expected to become the duke; he only took over when his elder brother, Karl II, was deposed. The two boys were the sons of Friedrich Wilhelm (who died at Quatre Bras) and grew up in exile from the duchy. Karl II succeeded as a child and took over the reins of government in 1823, when he was nineteen years old. He was not a popular duke, ignoring the constitution and doing nothing to rebuild the economy after the ravages of the Napoleonic Wars. By 1830 his subjects had had enough of him, and on 7 September they invaded and looted the schloss and burned it to the ground. Karl II was lucky to escape. His brother, Wilhelm, arrived a few days later and took over, initially on behalf of his brother but soon on his own account as duke. Karl II never forgave his brother for what he saw as a betrayal. The audio guide gives visitors the ability to drill down and listen to more detail about things they find interesting. I listened to a fascinating exchange of letters between the brothers in which they accuse and counter-accuse each other. Karl upbraids his brother for usurping his birthright and acting illegally, while Wilhelm retorts that it is his brother's entire fault and that Karl is not wanted in the duchy. Karl II took his case to court but lost, and Wilhelm went on to reign for over fifty years. He rebuilt the old Graue-Hof in a different, neoclassical, style.

Another helpful visitor aide in the museum are the family trees; these include pictures of each family member to help identify them, which is such a good idea. But there was one family member whom

I could not find anywhere at the schloss. She was not shown on the family tree and there was no portrait of her. Princess Caroline married George, Prince of Wales (the future George IV of Great Britain) in 1795 and was the last of four generations of Brunswick princesses who made grand marriages to emperors or kings (see chart 15). Caroline was later to acquire a scandalous reputation and perhaps this is why she has been left out. She was the queen of England who was refused admission to her coronation.

Little Richmond

Just a mile outside the centre of Braunschweig, along Wolfenbütteler Strasse, is a delightful summer pavilion set in a landscape park. Little Richmond was built for Duchess Augusta in the 1760s and named after Richmond Park in London to remind her of home.

Augusta was a British princess and the wife of Duke Karl Wilhelm Ferdinand. The schlösschen (little schloss) was her private retreat where she could amuse herself in the summer while her soldier husband was away campaigning. Built in baroque style, it was surrounded by a large English garden designed by Capability Brown.

We found Little Richmond with some difficulty. There were no signs and we just happened to spot the narrow entrance with gates that are embellished by a golden crown and the duchess's initial A. Little Richmond is small and charming and, unusual-

ly, is shaped like a diamond with the entrance at the bottom corner. The schlösschen is not open to the public and is apparently used as a venue for events. The park is open however, and has lovely views down to the river and the countryside beyond.

Caroline was the daughter of the celebrated soldier Duke Karl Friedrich Wilhelm. One theory is that his marriage in 1764 to Princess Augusta, the elder sister of George III, was arranged in compensation for the English king's failure to choose a Brunswick princess as his wife (George III had married Charlotte of Mecklenburg-Strelitz in 1761).[144] The marriage was not happy, and the couple had a tough time with their children. The duke spoke bitterly about arranged marriages which he blamed for inbreeding:

> The heart has nothing to do with these marriages, and the result is not only to embitter life, but to bring the most disastrous experience on those who come after.[145]

He was talking about his sons, three out of four of whom were mentally or physically handicapped. The duke and his wife also had two daughters, Caroline and her elder sister Augusta. Both had turbulent marriages that brought trouble to their parents. Augusta's husband was a wife beater and she eventually had to throw herself onto the mercy of Catherine the Great at the Russian court, where the couple lived.[146] Caroline's husband, George IV, would quickly come to loathe her and try desperately to get a divorce and prevent her from becoming queen.

What happened at the first meeting between the engaged couple, after Caroline's arrival in England, is well known. A visibly shocked Prince of Wales turned away from his bride-to-be, called for brandy, and left the room. Historians have tried to find something awful about Caroline that would account for this extreme reaction. It has been alleged that she was smelly due to poor personal hygiene or that she already had a notorious reputation for loose behaviour. I think the truth may be that it was not her fault, that George just didn't want to get married and would have reacted in much the same way whoever was the bride. He was in fact already married (although not officially) to a Catholic widow called Maria Fitzherbert and had agreed to a dynastic marriage only in order to squeeze money out of parliament to pay his debts. This strategy did not work, and George was soon faced by the reality of a wife he did not want and getting little extra money in return for what he saw as his sacrifice.

Caroline's reaction was to complain that her fiancé was fat and not as good looking as his portrait. She wasn't the girl to take things lying down, and this would be her usual reaction during the tribulations of their marriage. She thought it only right that she should stick up for herself and was fond of referring to the long tradition of soldiering in her family and saying that 'a Brunswicker never has been conquered yet.'[147]

53. Caroline of Brunswick arrives in Britain in 1795 to marry the prince of Wales.

Another of her reputed sayings must be one of history's snappiest:

My father was a hero. They married me to a zero.[148]

The newlyweds managed to cohabit briefly and nine months after the wedding, their daughter Charlotte was born; but after that they lived apart. George began a long campaign to exclude his wife from society, blacken her name, and get a divorce. He wanted to get rid of her as soon as possible, and he didn't want to meet her in the meantime. Living in seclusion wasn't Caroline's idea of what her life should be as princess of Wales, the second lady in the land, so she set up her own household and mini court in Blackheath just outside London. There were lots of rumours and innuendoes about the sort of life she lived there.

After her husband became prince regent (ruling in place of his de-ranged father, George III), the balance of power shifted further against Caroline, so she left England and went to live abroad. There she rel-ished her greater independence, lived more or less openly with a lover, travelled about as she pleased, and generally behaved in a way that was totally inappropriate for a princess of Wales at that time. George was increasingly desperate to cast her off; he had his wife secretly investi-gated and set spies on her, but he couldn't bring divorce proceedings without having to reveal his own adultery and even possibly, that pre-vious secret marriage. Caroline's poor treatment at the hands of her husband made her very popular with the general public (which George definitely was not), and she always had her political supporters.

When the prince regent became King George IV in January 1820, Caroline was still his wife and should therefore have become queen consort. The government tried to deny her the title and to buy her off to stay abroad, but she decided to return to Great Britain and claim her rights. She landed at the port of Dover in June to the cheers of the crowd and the thunder of a royal gun salute, and was carried to London on a sea of supporters. There the crowd celebrated with several days of rioting in the West End, pelting passersby with mud if they did not raise their hats to the queen and smashing the windows of houses that were not lit up in her support by candles in the windows.

But the government was moving against her, and a bill was soon in-troduced to the House of Lords that, if passed, would deprive Caroline of the rights and privileges of queen consort and divorce her from the king. The hearing of the bill began in August and effectively turned into Caroline's trial as a series of witnesses from the lower classes, some of them her ex-servants, gave evidence about her lifestyle abroad. They had all been paid to come and most of what they said was tittle-tattle even if it was true; some of it was perjury and discounted in cross-examination. Caroline's lawyers could not prove her innocent of adultery, but the government's case was tainted by its methods of obtaining evidence. In November the bill was withdrawn and she was acquitted.

The Fate of Schlösser in the Twentieth Century

The twentieth century presented a grave threat to the survival of schlösser. Four years of gruelling conflict had destroyed the fabric of pre-World War I society when revolution toppled the German monarchy in November 1918. Without their ruling princes these large buildings lost the main purposes for which they were designed—to be representative symbols of power and centres of administration as well as royal family homes. Some remained in the family ownership and were opened as museums, including Bückeburg; others, such as Saalfeld, were taken over by the local government and became offices; many entered into a long period of decline.

Worse was to follow in World War II, as schlösser were damaged by bombing or destroyed by fire. These included Herrenhausen, which was the German ancestral home of the British royal family (see Schloss I). Over the seventy years since the end of the war, many have been restored or rebuilt, but some, such as Neustrelitz, seem lost forever due to lack of money. Kiel Schloss was one of the first to be reconstructed, in the 1960s. In keeping with the mood of the times, it was rebuilt as a modern block. One of the latest to rise from the ashes is Braunschweig, which opened in 2007. Due to the enormous cost, only the front of the new schloss is a replica of the old.

A further challenge in this difficult century fell to those schlösser behind the Iron Curtain when Germany was divided after World War II. These were expropriated and used as institutions, including barracks, refugee camps, old people's homes, schools, sanatoriums, hospitals, prisons, and even interrogation centres. With their contents dissipated and their interiors altered, they suffered neglect and deterioration for nearly fifty years. But this is a relatively short time in the history of these buildings and many have already been restored and opened as museums, including Mirow and Rheinsberg.

In the twenty-first century the challenge remains—to find a commercial use and be self-supporting. The list of schlösser in appendix B includes their current use. While many are secure as museums, hotels, or government offices, others are still struggling to find funding or a commercial venture to guarantee their survival, including Reinhardsbrunn.

The coronation of George IV was on 19 July 1821. This had been delayed from the previous summer because of the Queen Caroline affair. George had no intention of allowing his wife to be crowned (which was within his prerogative), and he made sure she was not even invited to the ceremony at Westminster Abbey. Caroline made a last attempt to assert her rights, driving to the abbey with her attendants and, at the door, demanding entry as of right as the queen of England. She was turned away because she did not show a ticket. She must have already been seriously ill, but after this she lost the will to live and died less than a month later. By her own wish her body was taken home and buried in Braunschweig Cathedral.

Caroline is one of the most colourful British queens and the popular press had a field day with her story. Here is one of the best-remembered ditties about her:

> O Gracious Queen we thee implore
> To go away and sin no more.
> Or, if the effort be too great,
> To go away at any rate.[149]

Wolfenbüttel

Schloss Wolfenbüttel looks very impressive, although it was difficult for us to see it properly as it was obscured by the paraphernalia of a travelling funfair in the palace square. The front elevation is painted a dark rusty pink and is decorated with pilasters, garlands, and carved stone figures. The schloss is surrounded by a moat, and separating this from the square is an elaborate stone parapet ornamented with more stone figures and huge urns. The entrance is over a bridge across the moat and through a magnificent triumphal arch, above which hangs a huge coat of arms. It is all very grand and imposing indeed.

Once through the vaulted entrance passageway and into the cobbled internal courtyard however, there is a very different feeling.

Shaded by a pair of trees growing in the middle, this is unostentatious and tranquil and was my favourite part of the schloss. Perhaps it was the open arcade running around the courtyard at ground floor level, rather like a cloister. Originally this was two stories high, but the upper floor was filled in at the end of the seventeenth century and has windows and half-timbered walls painted red, white, and yellow. Schloss Wolfenbüttel is a very large building but it seems to be well used. As well as the museum, the schloss is home to a theatre, a cultural centre, and a high school.

54. The grand entrance at Wolfenbüttel is across the bridge and through a triumphal arch; the little boat in the moat was part of a travelling funfair.

At the top of the staircase to the museum we were greeted by a large banner advertising a special exhibition commemorating the three-hundred-year anniversary of the death of Duke Anton Ulrich of Brunswick-Wolfenbüttel (1633–1714). He is one of my favourite royal characters from the tour. Anton Ulrich was the middle of three sons and, as seems to have been usual at the time, he and his brothers squabbled over their inheritance. After their father's death in 1666, a separate principality of Brunswick-Bevern was created for the youngest son. Anton Ulrich and his elder brother ruled jointly over the remainder until the brother's death in 1704, and then Anton Ulrich was sole duke until his own death in 1714. He therefore had a close hand in the affairs of the duchy for going on fifty years.

The exhibition was entitled *The Sun in the North*, reflecting that Anton Ulrich was one of the best-known personalities of his age. Perhaps the title is to compare him to his contemporary, Louis XIV of France (1638–1715), who is known as the Sun King. During the long reign of Anton Ulrich, Wolfenbüttel blossomed into a baroque cultural centre that was known well beyond its borders. This was where Johanna Elizabeth of Anhalt-Zerbst brought her young daughter Sophie (later Catherine the Great) to polish her up for the royal marriage market.[150] The duke was a connoisseur and great art collector who visited Italy several times. He wrote poetry and also novels that were thinly disguised accounts of stories from real life. When each instalment came out, there would be a rash of letters between the royal courts trying to identify the characters.

There is a portrait of Anton Ulrich at Wolfenbüttel that I was very much taken with. It was painted in 1695, when he would have been sixty-one or sixty-two years old. He is dressed in the height of fashion, with a triple bow of pink silk around his neck and enormous hair. Cascades of brown, puffed-up curls flow down over his shoulders and reach almost to his waist (this would have been a wig of course). He looks straight at the viewer with a confident gaze and a slightly mischievous smile. For despite all his talents and his fame, Anton Ulrich was jealous of his cousins in the Brunswick-Lüneburg branch of the family and not above meddling in their affairs.

A good example is the trouble caused when Ernst August of Calenberg decided to introduce primogeniture in the Brunswick-Lüneburg branch of the family. Duke Ernst August was the youngest of the four dukes of Brunswick-Lüneburg, whose fascinating story I wrote about in my first book (see Celle in *Schloss I*). By now only two of the four were still alive, Ernst August and his elder brother Georg Wilhelm, and Ernst August was due to inherit from his brother under an agreement the two had made many years before. He was lobbying to be promoted to elector of the Holy Roman Empire and knew his case would be stronger if he ended the family tradition whereby two sons in each generation inherited. On Christmas Day 1684 he told his family of his decision to introduce primogeniture and asked his younger sons to sign an agreement giving up their rights. Understandably, his second son, Friedrich August, who saw himself disinherited at a stroke, refused. Enter Anton Ulrich.

Anton Ulrich championed the cause of Friedrich August, giving him shelter at Schloss Wolfenbüttel and helping him to draft a legal claim against his father. This didn't work; in return, Ernst August repudiated his son and cut off his allowance. Poor Friedrich August was forced to become a mercenary and died fighting the Turks only a few years later in 1690, aged twenty-nine. And sadly the pattern was then repeated with Ernst August's third son, Maximilian. He had previously accepted the change but now, with Anton Ulrich's support, took up his dead brother's position. The old conspiracy was revived, and a coup d'état to topple Ernst August was planned.[151] But the plot was given away, and Maximilian and his co-conspirers were arrested. One of them was executed, but Maximilian and the rest were released. Maximilian left his father's court and joined the army of the Holy Roman emperor, where he rose to be a field marshal. He never gave up hope of regaining his inheritance.[152]

In 1692 Ernst August achieved his ambition to gain an electoral vote and became the elector of Hannover. It must have galled Anton Ulrich that his cousin from the junior branch of the family now out-ranked him. But he could also outshine by the splendour of his palace at Salzdahlum.

Salzdahlum

Anton Ulrich was an enthusiastic builder and, in the village of Salzdahlum on the outskirts of Wolfenbüttel, the Sun in the North built his own version of Louis XIV's Versailles. Old prints show it to have been a magnificent baroque schloss surrounded by acres and acres of amazing formal gardens. Salzdahlum was built for show and was the backdrop for grand occasions. This was where Anton Ulrich received Peter the Great of Russia in 1713 and where Frederick the Great of Prussia married Elisabeth Christine of Brunswick-Wolfenbüttel in the famous double marriage of 1733.

Salzdahlum was built during the years 1688–1694, but Anton Ulrich was continually adding new extensions right up until his death in 1714, especially additional galleries which he needed to house his vast and ever-growing art collection. Much of this can still be seen today in the Herzog Anton Ulrich Art Gallery in Braunschweig.

The schloss was built as a summer palace and, to save money, it was constructed mainly out of wood which was then disguised as stone. This was why it was always cold in winter. I have a wonderful visual picture of Anton Ulrich and the Electress Sophia of Hannover (widow of his old adversary Ernst August), he in his seventies and she in her eighties, dancing down the freezing galleries at Salzdahlum to keep warm, followed by Anton Ulrich's aged pug dog called Mops, from which he was inseparable.[153]

The timber construction did not stand the test of time. Only a century after Anton Ulrich's death, Salzdahlum was in a very poor condition and the gardens overgrown. It was torn down and the garden levelled in the years 1811–1813, when Brunswick-Wolfenbüttel was part of the kingdom of Westphalia. We went to the village and found a plaque on the old gatehouse, which is the only part of the schloss remaining and is now a private house.

We enjoyed our visit to the museum in Schloss Wolfenbüttel, even though their policy of no photographs was a disappointment and we apparently missed the arrival of the new English audio guide by a week! The ducal apartments are shown very much as they would have been in the time of Anton Ulrich and the two sons who ruled after him. I particularly liked the Audience Chamber with its red damask walls, where he sat on a throne under a red velvet canopy, flanked by two larger-than-life Moorish figures that were given to him by Tsar Peter the Great when he visited Salzdahlum.[154] Also favourites were the Inlaid Cabinet room in the duchess's apartments, where the walls are lined with precious panels inlaid with luxury woods and ivory, and the First Anteroom next door, with oval portraits of the three granddaughters of Anton Ulrich.

In his old age, Anton Ulrich channelled his ambition into the marriages of these three granddaughters, and thus began the series of great matches for princesses of Brunswick-Wolfenbüttel that would go on through the next four generations until the family died out (see chart 15). It kicked off in 1708 when the eldest of the three, Elisabeth Christine, made a very grand marriage indeed to the future Holy Roman Emperor Karl VI of Austria. She was forced to convert to Catholicism against her inclination and her life would be blighted by her failure to produce a male heir, but she lived to see her husband change the rules of succession so that her daughter, Maria Theresa, would become the reigning empress of Austria. This caused a lot of trouble around the courts of Europe and sparked off the War of the Austrian Succession (1740–1748) when Karl died.

The youngest of the three was Antoinette Amalie; she secured the family line and reunited their lands when in 1712 she married Anton Ulrich's nephew, Ferdinand Albrecht II of Brunswick-Bevern. He was the son of that younger brother for whom this separate principality had been created in 1666. Anton Ulrich was succeeded by each of his two surviving sons in turn, but neither had a son of his own, and Ferdinand Albrecht was the next heir. In contrast to her eldest sister, Antoinette Amalie produced six sons and six daughters who lived to grow up, including two future queens.

But it is the marriage of the middle daughter, Charlotte Christine, that I find the most interesting. In 1711 she achieved a first when she

55. The Little Palace at Wolfenbüttel was once the residence of the hereditary crown prince.

married the only son of Tsar Peter the Great, Grand Duke Alexei Petrovich. Up until that time all members of the Russian royal house had married women from the Russian nobility. Russia was regarded as an un-civilised, backward, and crude country by the cultured and mannered courts of Europe, and the reaction was generally shock at the engagement and pity for the bride. The Prussian king, Friedrich I, said he would never dream of sending a child into such a barbaric country.[155]

Alexei had a very bad relationship with his father and opposed the tsar's policy of westernising Russia. Because Charlotte Christine was the choice of his father, the marriage was probably doomed from the start. Charlotte Christine died in St Petersburg in 1715, aged twenty-one, a few days after giving birth to her second child. The relationship between Alexei and his father spiralled even further downward, and Alexei fled abroad and sought the protection of Karl VI, the husband of his dead wife's elder sister. He was lured back to Russia and died under torture in 1718.

Sometime after Charlotte Christine's death, the legend grew up that she had not died at all but escaped to happiness and a new life in Louisiana. This inspired the German writer Heinrich Zschokke (1771–1848) to write a novel called *The Princess of Brunswick-Wolfenbüttel*.[156] The story opens in 1714 in St Petersburg, where the princess has just given birth to her first child. Lonely, isolated, and rejected by her husband, she bemoans the lot of princesses in arranged marriages:

We, decked out like eastern slaves, are given to such powerful beings as demand us: state policy signs the contract, and our broken hearts are turned into merchandise.[157]

Denied any hope of a separation, which her parents and the tsar will not hear of, the princess decides to fake her own death and plans this during her second pregnancy, with the help of some devoted servants. After the birth she acts out her deathbed scene, even lying in state in her open coffin with a veil over her face. As the coffin is closed she is hidden in the palace and then secretly spirited away dressed as a boy.

After various adventures she eventually ends up in a fictional New World settlement called Christinenthal in Louisiana, where she falls in love and makes a happy marriage to a commoner. At the end of the novel the princess returns as a widow to live quietly in Europe. The Brunswick-Wolfenbüttel family pay her a pension but keep the secret of her existence forever.

Kaiserpfalz Goslar

There is a legend in Germany that Emperor Friedrich Barbarossa is asleep inside the Kyffhäuser mountain in Thuringia. The emperor died by drowning in 1190, attempting to cross a river while on crusade. But in the legend he is waiting in the mountain, and outside evil ravens circle overhead. One day, according to the prophecy, the ravens will disappear and the emperor will wake up and emerge to herald in a new golden age.[158] This legend is depicted in one of the large wall paintings in the Imperial Hall at Kaiserpfalz Goslar. Here, as the ravens are being scattered by the imperial eagle, the old emperor steps out of his cave. He points across the hall to the painting in which Kaiser Wilhelm I is being offered the crown of the new German empire. The symbolism and the message are clear. Here is my successor, who will restore the glory of the German empire!

56 Kaiserpfalz Goslar was one of more than one hundred imperial palaces used by the Holy Roman emperors.

Kaiserpfalz Goslar was built in the first years of the eleventh century and was one of more than one hundred imperial palaces used by the Holy Roman emperors, including Friedrich Barbarossa. These early emperors did not reside in a single place but 'ruled from the back of a horse',[159] constantly travelling around their territory and stopping for a few days here and there to hold court. Goslar was chosen as the location for one of these stopping places because the nearby silver mines had made it prosperous. The first imperial court was held there in 1009, the last in 1253. After that the building fell into decay and was used for lots of different purposes, including as a barn for storage. By the nineteenth century, it was tumbling down and falling apart.

It would probably have disappeared altogether had it not been bought by the kingdom of Hannover in 1866. The price agreed was nominal (around €1,500), but more importantly there was a clause in the contract obliging the new owner to restore the schloss. When Prussia annexed Hannover later in the same year, the new Prussian owners honoured the contract, and Goslar was preserved. After the formation of the German Empire in 1871, it acquired even more significance as a symbol of nationalism and past imperial glory. The idea to turn the bare walls into a painted history book came from Crown Prince Friedrich of Prussia during a visit to Goslar with his father, Kaiser Wilhelm I, in 1875.

The historical paintings at Goslar are the work of the artist Hermann Wislicenus, and they took him eighteen years to complete (from 1879 to 1897). There are sixty-seven of them in total, including the eleven huge paintings that tell the story of the empire from the Middle Ages to modern times. Colourful, glowing, and painted in grand heroic style, these paintings are quite extraordinary. They present an imaginary and romantic view of history in which real events are interwoven with legends and fairy tales. The series begins with the story of the Sleeping Beauty, the princess in the fairy tale who is waiting to be woken by her prince's kiss. Like the legend of Friedrich Barbarossa, she

57. Kaiser Wilhelm I and his son, Crown Prince Friedrich,
visited Goslar in 1875.

171

is another symbol for Germany's sleeping greatness. The climax of the story is told in the last painting in the series, in which Kaiser Wilhelm I is offered the imperial crown. This is the largest painting in the hall and it occupies the central position. It depicts not only real people who were present at the actual event in the Hall of Mirrors in Versailles palace, but also long-dead Prussian ancestors and allegorical figures. So here are Chancellor Bismarck, who engineered the birth of the empire, and King Ludwig II of Bavaria, who proffered the crown on behalf of the other German princes (he did it only to make sure of secret subsidies from Prussia to fund his schloss-building programme). But in the picture too are Father Rhine and two female figures representing the provinces of Alsace and Lorraine, recently taken from France by Prussia. The figure of Legend holds an open book, which reads,

> And when the emperor of old emerges from his cave, the thorn rose will bloom and the empire will prosper.

The Kaiserpfalz is a large building consisting of two big meeting rooms, one on each floor, with a church added on at one end. The two meeting rooms were used by the emperors to hold court and for other government and representational purposes. Their living quarters were in separate buildings nearby. On the first floor the Imperial Hall, which houses the historical paintings, is 147 feet long and 49 feet wide. It has large windows that in the emperors' time would have been open to the elements (today they are glazed), so this hall could only be used in summer. Downstairs in the Winter Hall there are smaller windows and a rudimentary heating system, making this more suitable for use in winter.

The lower floor today houses the Vaults Museum, about the history of the Holy Roman Empire and the Goslar emperors. I thought the curators had done a good job here as everything is well laid out. I enjoyed a happy half hour browsing in the emperors gallery, which has a storyboard with a portrait of and brief information about each of the Holy

Roman emperors of the Goslar period (those who ruled during the 250 years that Goslar was an imperial palace). They include Heinrich III, who ruled from 1039–1056 and was the Holy Roman emperor who really put imperial Goslar on the map.[160] He rebuilt the Kaiserpfalz into the structure we see today, and it became his favourite palace which he visited twenty-three times. His son, the future Heinrich IV (1056–1106), was born at Goslar in 1050, and when he died Heinrich III directed that his heart be buried there. The emperors gallery also includes Friedrich I, known as Barbarossa (or red beard), who was emperor from 1155 until his death in 1190.

The portraits of these medieval emperors are taken from old coins, manuscript illustrations, and tombs. They were never intended to be true likenesses, but rather as badges or symbols to represent their high office. Each emperor is portrayed sitting on a throne or with the insignia of his position—the crown, the sceptre, and the orb. The concept of an individual portrait, showing the features of the subject, did not arrive until after the Goslar period.[161]

The centrepiece of the Vaults Museum is the imperial throne, which dates back to the reign of Heinrich IV. This is splendidly displayed inside a large metal cage designed to give the impression of a medieval cathedral (it is difficult to describe this, but it is very effective). The bronze throne was made using local metals and consists of the upper part, which sat on a stone base; the outside of the back and sides

58. Emperor Friedrich Barbarossa stands guard outside Goslar.

are intricately and beautifully carved with vines, fruit, and flowers, and the assumption is that it was padded with cushions on the inside to make it more comfortable.[162] This amazing piece of workmanship is nearly a thousand years old! But my favourite exhibit in the museum was a little bird that sat on top of the roof of the Kaiserpfalz for seven hundred years. Also made from local metals, this is a griffin, a mythological bird that symbolises wealth because of the small round piece of gold it carries in its mouth.

Kaiserpfalz Goslar is clearly a popular stop for the tour buses and there were coach parties arriving on the hour. Our own arrival coincided with one of these which made the lady on the ticket desk rather flustered, but she still found time to deal with us and search out some information in English. The two big meeting rooms are laid out with rows of seats and microphones for the coach parties and their guides to use. But the crowds and the commentary did not interfere with our enjoyment; the Kaiserpfalz is large and there is plenty of room for everyone. This is a fun place to visit.

Wolfsburg

In Lower Saxony we stayed in Wolfsburg, which is known to all Germans as the Volkswagen town because it is home to the company's headquarters. Our hotel was in an unusual complex called Autostadt (Car City), which is next to the Volkswagen factory and is a theme park for their cars. Here, in ultramodern architecture and set among over sixty acres of pristine and manicured gardens and lakes, there are museums, shops, cinemas, cafes, and other attractions, all devoted to the motorcar. From our bedroom window at night we looked out on illuminated glass towers, two hundred feet tall, full of new Volkswagen cars.

It was a strange place to stay, but the hotel staff could not have been kinder or more eager to make our stay a success. Most of the other guests were either business visitors to Volkswagen or customers who had come to pick up their new cars. When buying a new car, many Germans like to make an occasion of it and travel to Autostadt with their families to take delivery with zero miles on the clock (the odometer). So we were a novelty in the hotel because we were sightseers. The staff became intrigued with our interest in schlösser and questioned us each evening about our progress. On our last night the chefs created a special dessert for me as a surprise. On top of this were two circular, clear, sugar discs, each encasing a photo of their local schloss at Wolfsburg. It was one of the nicest surprise presents I have ever received.

59. Each padlock on the chain at Wolfsburg commemorates
a wedding that took place there.

Around 1300, the lords of Bartensleben began building a castle in the meadows of the River Aller to guard the river crossing. Schloss Wolfsburg took its name (the Wolf's Castle) from the Bartensleben family coat of arms, which is a wolf leaping over two sheaves of corn. Six centuries later (in 1945), the schloss would give its name to the city of Wolfsburg. The original castle was a fortified keep, but by 1622 the family had rebuilt it into a Renaissance palace with four wings around

an internal courtyard, in accordance with the trend in schloss building at the time. This area was the border between the electorate of
Hannover and the duchy of Brunswick-Wolfenbüttel, but from 1680
Wolfsburg was an enclave of the electorate of Brandenburg (later the
kingdom of Prussia). In 1718 the schloss passed into the ownership
of the Schulenburg-Wolfsburg line when the last of the Bartensleben
family, Anna Adelheit Catharina, married Graf Adolph Friedrich von
der Schulenburg. Schloss Wolfsburg remained in the ownership of the
descendants of Adolph and Anna until Graf Günther was forced to sell
it when the city of Wolfsburg was founded.

The Schulenburgs were a noble family who served the electors and
kings of Prussia with distinction for several generations. The family
can be dated back to the twelfth century, but it was Graf Gustav Adolph
(1632–1691) and his children who brought the family to prominence.
Gustav Adolph rose to be a Brandenburg privy councillor; his eldest
son, Johann Matthias (1661–1747), became a field marshal in the Vene-
tian army; and his daughter, Melusine (1667–1743), also became famous
as the mistress of George I of Great Britain. *Schloss I* includes the story
of George's marriage to his cousin Sophie Dorothee of Celle and of her
long-term incarceration under house arrest at Ahlden following their
divorce. His affair with Melusine started during his marriage and lasted
until his death, and it is possible that they secretly married (in a morganatic marriage), perhaps after his ex-wife's death in 1726.[163] George and
Melusine had three daughters together, the youngest of which married
Graf Albrecht Wolfgang of Schaumburg-Lippe (see Bückeburg).

Adolph Friedrich (1685–1741), the first Schulenburg at Wolfsburg,
was the son of Melusine's and Johann Matthias's sister Margarete
Gertrud, who had married a cousin also called Schulenburg. Adolph
Friedrich was another family member who had a distinguished career
in the service of the kings of Prussia. He was a trusted adviser to King
Friedrich Wilhelm I and commanded the king's famous regiment of
specially recruited tall infantry soldiers known as the Lange Kerls, or
Long Fellows.[164] He was also president of the military court that tried

Frederick the Great and his friend von Katte after Frederick's abortive attempt to run away from his father (see Schloss Rheinsberg).[165] Adolf Friedrich seems to have carried out this difficult task with caution and some skill. The court committed Frederick to his father's mercy (he was detained under strict conditions) and passed a sentence of life imprisonment on von Katte (Friedrich Wilhelm changed this to the death sentence). After Friedrich Wilhelm's death, Adolph Friedrich was not in such high favour with the new king and wanted to retire. But Frederick refused his resignation, and Adolf Friedrich was killed in 1741 at the Battle of Mollwitz during the War of the Austrian Succession, which was Frederick's first battle as king.

Today Schloss Wolfsburg is owned by the City of Wolfsburg and is used as a cultural centre and museum of art. The schloss is also a wedding venue and we thought the chains of wedding padlocks on the bridge over the moat were a very nice touch. Each of these brightly coloured padlocks commemorates a wedding and has the name or initials of the bride and groom and the date.

In an outbuilding of the schloss is a museum about the history of Wolfsburg—the town as well as the castle. The contents of this were thought provoking. It was Adolf Hitler who asked the auto engineer Ferdinand Porsche to design an affordable car for the masses and Hitler who laid the foundation stone of a factory to produce it in 1938, on land that had been part of the estate of the Grafs von Schulenburg-Wolfsburg. There is a photograph of this event in the museum. The car was called the KdF-Wagen, and the new town was given the same name; the Stadt (town) des KdF-Wagen. The initials stand for Kraft durch Freude, or Strength through Joy. The car would later become popularly known as the Volkswagen Beetle, and it would be the most successful car of all time. Without the Beetle there would be no Wolfsburg.

During World War II the Wolfsburg factory manufactured armaments using forced and slave labour from prisoner-of-war camps and also, presumably, local concentration camps. It had been intended that factory workers would live in model housing in a new garden city, but these plans had to be set aside because of the war. Conditions in the factories in the war years must have been appalling, but there is little about this period in the museum. After the war the British occupying forces insisted that the town be renamed, so it took the name of the schloss—Wolfsburg. Refugees from East Germany and immigrants from Italy and other countries poured into Wolfsburg, seeking a new life. And only ten years later, in 1955, the one millionth Beetle rolled off the production line. The museum has exhibits showing life in Wolfsburg during the post-war years of the German economic miracle, including the entire fittings of a hairdressing salon from the 1950s. The town's prosperity today is still founded on Volkswagen and the auto industry. It has the highest per capita income, making it the richest city in Germany.

The two museum attendants at Wolfsburg did not speak much English but warmed to our interest and did their best to help us. They also told us there was another schloss in the city and strongly recommended that we visit this. It was late in the afternoon on a public holiday, and we wondered whether it would still be open when we got there. But the Wolfsburg attendants were insistent, going to the trouble of phoning ahead to check opening times and get the street name for our satellite navigation. You will definitely like Schloss Fallersleben, they told us. And we did—very much.

Fallersleben

It was a lovely surprise to arrive at Fallersleben and find ourselves in the middle of a country fete. We were greeted by the sound of live music on the green just outside the schloss. There was a band playing and a male choir singing traditional German songs. They all looked very smart, dressed in the same uniform of white trousers, dark jacket, and a naval captain's peaked cap. The locals were out enjoying themselves in the late afternoon spring sunshine, and the stalls on the green were doing a brisk trade in beer and German food. In the castle lake a fountain played, and on the bridge across the dry moat there were pots of red geraniums nodding cheerfully. Inside the schloss it was busy too, with crowds of people milling around in the small rooms. We had come on only the second day of a brand-new exhibition about the German national anthem.

60. At Fallersleben there was a brand-new exhibition about the German National Anthem.

The reason why this exhibition is in Schloss Fallersleben is that the anthem, which is called 'The Song of Germany', was written by the town's most famous son. Heinrich Hoffman was a popular poet and songwriter who called himself Hoffman von Fallersleben, after his hometown. Hoffman was born in 1798, at a time when the old order in Germany was being challenged by the new French Republic. As a child he experienced the Napoleonic Wars first hand, when different armies marched back and forth through Fallersleben, and for a time it was under foreign rule as part of the French dominated kingdom of Westphalia. As a student he became a liberal and a nationalist and was deeply disappointed that the old order of patchwork principalities was re-established at the end of the wars. He tramped round Germany on foot writing satirical poetry and political songs; the exhibition called him the Singing Agitator. When he wrote 'The Song of Germany' in 1841, it was a subversive song that called for German unification and democratic freedoms. The third verse expresses his political ideas; it is the only verse used today.

> Unity and justice and freedom
> For the German fatherland.
> Let us all strive for this purpose
> Brotherly with heart and hand.
> Unity and justice and freedom
> Are the pledge of happiness,
> Bloom in the glow of happiness,
> Bloom, German Fatherland!

'The Song of Germany' has always been a controversial song. It was first chosen to be the German national anthem by the Weimar Republic, after the end of the German monarchy. Later it would be readopted by West Germany after World War II, and again after German reunification in 1990. But only the third verse would be used, as the first two were no longer thought politically correct. The first verse, which includes the line 'Deutschland, Deutschland über alles', is too closely associated with the Nazis (it was a surprise to me that this line is not actually in the German national anthem). The second verse, which talks about wine, women, and song, is too chauvinistic and more like a drinking song.

The exhibition makes the point that even after 1990, many Germans were ambivalent about their national flag and anthem, seeing these as tainted by the country's problematic history. It puts the turning point at 2006, when Germany hosted the Football World Cup and football fans began to sport their national colours of black, red, and gold and proudly sing 'The Song of Germany'.

61. The band was playing and a choir singing on
the green at Fallersleben.

I want to heartily congratulate Schloss Fallersleben for a beautifully
laid-out and very interesting exhibition. The story of the life, work,
and times of Hoffman von Fallersleben is told in an imaginative and
innovative way. There are lots of visual aids for the visitor to enjoy,
including an illustrated timeline of key events and an unusual map of
Germany in which a series of different-coloured transparencies can
be overlaid to see the political structure at different dates (1806, 1871,
1990...). A further novelty is a karaoke machine that allows visitors to
sing the anthem themselves and then hear it played back. This was
very popular and there was a happy background of singing and laugh-
ing, so inside the schloss it felt like a continuation of the holiday mood
outside. There was also plenty of English translation on the displays.
There is something in this museum for all ages and nationalities.

The schloss at Fallersleben is a very pretty building that is half-
timbered on a stone base and painted pink. It is quite modest and more
like a manor house or large farmhouse than a palace. There were once
three wings in a horseshoe shape around an open courtyard, but only
one wing now survives, together with the staircase tower and a cavalier
house. The schloss was built in the first half of the sixteenth century

and its most famous resident was Duchess Clara of Saxe-Lauenburg, who was the widow of Duke Franz of Brunswick-Lüneburg. After her husband's death in 1549, Schloss Fallersleben was her widow's dower and she lived there for nearly thirty years until her own death in 1576. Duchess Clara enlarged the schloss, introduced new coinage, and created a thriving local economy.[166] From the mid-seventeenth century, Schloss Fallersleben ceased to be a ducal residence and was used for various purposes of local government. Recently it has been completely renovated and refurbished for the new permanent exhibition. And this time our luck was in—having visited Mirow a month before their new museum was due to open and Wolfenbüttel a week before their English audio guide arrived, we timed it right at Fallersleben. We visited the day after the schloss museum reopened.

8

REFLECTIONS

A nd so our schloss tour, which began at beautiful Bückeburg, came to an end on a sunny afternoon in jolly Fallersleben, with the band playing, the beer tent in full swing, and the exhibition in the schloss packed with visitors. It was a fitting way to finish off a wonderful trip. For three weeks we had explored the northern half of Germany, having adventures, enjoying the food, and visiting some stunning places. If this is the sort of thing you like doing too, then why not go schloss hunting in Germany?

My husband and I call it schloss hunting because of the problem we encountered early on—there is simply no comprehensive list of schlösser that visitors can use, even those that are open to the public. For our main source of information we used two books about palaces and castles (called *Time To Travel: Travel in Time* and *Schencks Castles and Gardens*[167]), but not all of the schlösser we visited are included in these. We soon discovered it was important to keep our eyes open and follow up leads locally, as this could take us to some of the most interesting places. A recommendation in the tourist information office took us to Rastede, a leaflet in German to Jever, and an inaccurate reference in our German guidebook to Reinhardsbrunn.

Schloss hunting gave us many adventures and led us to all sorts of different locations, from the centre of the auto industry at Wolfsburg in the industrial heartland of West Germany to Rheinsberg (across unmade roads through sleepy villages) in the deep countryside of what was once East Germany, behind the Iron Curtain. And at the end, there were often surprises—as well as visiting schlösser that are open to the public as museums, we found ourselves in a schloss that is now a shopping precinct (Braunschweig), a concert hall (Kiel), and the local motor tax office (Saalfeld). Where we knew little of the schloss beforehand and had no expectations, we often had the best visits.

Germany is an extremely beautiful country and large parts of it are unknown to British visitors. Our journey for this book took us through some varied and picturesque scenery ranging from the seascapes of Schleswig-Holstein to the lakes and marshland of Mecklenburg-Western Pomerania and the wooded hills of the Thuringian forest. From touring the countryside to visit schlösser, I have learnt a lot about the geography of Germany.

I have discovered too that it is a country with a fascinating history that has followed a very different path from our own. Should you look on the shelves in a British bookshop, you will probably find that the majority of books on German history are about the twentieth century, particularly the Nazi period. This was a turbulent and terrible time, but it did not last long in historical terms (only twelve years). There will be few, if any, books on earlier centuries or about the Holy Roman Empire of the German Nation that lasted over eight hundred years. And there are not nearly enough books written in English, or translated from the German, about Germany's royal families.

It was the chance finding of a portrait of Queen Victoria in our attic that originally sparked my interest in the history of royalty. I wasn't interested in history at all at school. But from reading up about Victoria's colourful life story, I discovered that history, when seen through the eyes of the personal stories of princes and princesses, makes compelling reading. And from visiting schlösser, I learnt that seeing the places where these royal families lived brings their stories more vividly to life. I hope this book may play a part in convincing you of this.

Royal lives can also tell us a lot about the times in which they lived, and some common threads run through many of the stories in this book. Arranged marriages linked Europe's royal families together in an exclusive network that secured dynastic interests and perpetuated the monarchical system, but this came at a cost to the happiness and well-being of individual royals, particularly princesses. And how to pass the inheritance on to the next generation was always a problem; the introduction of primogeniture, brought in to secure the family power base and keep their lands intact, also had a downside for some family members, this time younger sons.

The schlösser included in this book were built over many centuries and in different architectural styles. They include the eleventh-century Kaiserpfalz at Goslar, built to house the travelling court of a peripatetic Holy Roman emperor; the West Wing at Heidecksburg, remodelled in the mid-eighteenth century in fantastic rococo style; and the neoclassical Residenzschloss at Weimar, built at the beginning of the nineteenth century to provide a fit home for the daughter of a Russian emperor. From understanding the history of these wonderful buildings and the different architectural styles, we came to appreciate their adaptability and durability. Over the centuries schlösser have survived war, fire, and neglect and were continually rebuilt or remodelled to meet the changing needs and fashions of the day. The twentieth century probably brought the greatest challenges when the end of the monarchy took away their prime purpose and started a decline in the fortunes of many, particularly for those that would be behind the Iron Curtain for nearly fifty years. Many have reinvented themselves as museums, hotels, and government offices; but others such as Reinhardsbrunn are struggling to find an owner and commercial use.

In England we have a TV programme called *The Hotel Inspector*, in which a successful hotelier visits other hotels and gives them advice on how to improve. After visiting twenty-five schlösser in a relatively short time, I almost feel I could be *The Schloss Inspector*, commenting on the schloss experience from the point of view of a foreign visitor. If I were, my advice would fall into three main areas.

The first area might be loosely termed the practicalities. That may sound trivial but these things are important. Very often we had difficulty in finding the schloss and had to stop and ask directions. Clear signs showing how to get to there and where to park would be a great help to visitors. Visiting schlösser is a delightful occupation but it can be tiring, so it is always a plus if there is a good coffee shop, or at least if the attendants can recommend one nearby. The inconsistent rules about taking photographs are an irritant for visitors—in some places I could take pictures freely; in others I had to buy a photo permit; and in some schlösser the policy was no photos at all. It was never made clear (with one exception) why there needed to be restrictions. And I am sure there must be a better solution to protecting precious floors than asking visitors to risk an accident by wearing precipitous felt overshoes.

The Schloss Inspector – Dos and Don'ts

- Clear directions to the schloss
- Innovative methods of display
- Label the family portraits
- Translation into English
- Welcoming and friendly staff
- A good coffee shop is a plus

- No slippery felt overshoes
- No restrictions on taking photos
- No unhelpful bureaucracy
- Don't forget the historical personal stories
- Don't herd visitors on a rehearsed patter tour
- Don't treat us like interlopers

The second area of my advice would be about how the museum contents are presented to attract the visitor's attention. There were some schlösser that may be missing a trick by concentrating almost entirely on the building and the decoration and leaving out the historical personal stories. We saw some excellent examples of curating, such as the karaoke machine at Fallersleben, the storyboard for each of the Goslar Holy Roman emperors, and the illustrated family trees at Braunschweig. These kinds of innovative presentations tend to work well even for non-German-speaking visitors.

However to make visiting the schloss a good experience for foreign visitors, there does need to be translated material and, as the most widely spoken, English is the obvious choice of language for this. While some schlösser did provide high-quality information translated into English (for example, the excellent English guidebooks at Eutin and Bückeburg), in others it was skimpy and pedestrian. And in those schlösser where entry is restricted to the mandatory guided tour, the foreign visitor experience depends entirely on how good the guide is and whether or not he or she speaks English.

But my third area is the most important, as the visitor's experience depends more on it than any other factor. This is the attitude and approach of the museum attendants. This matters more than whether the schloss is smart or shabby, how the exhibits are laid out, or whether there is material in English. In most cases our experience was positive and we had a warm welcome from knowledgeable and friendly staff who helped us to enjoy our visit. But in a few cases it was not.

From the twenty-five schlösser we saw I have some favourites, each for different reasons. Eutin is a favourite for the wonderful collection of royal portraits, and Burg Stargard for the happy experience of a spring morning spent exploring an interesting Brick Gothic fortress. Belvedere stays in my mind as a perfect jewel of a schloss, with a strong association to a Russian grand duchess who built a garden there to remind her of home. Rheinsberg appeals because it has an atmospheric feeling of a lost age, and was where the enthralling historical story of two talented but difficult brothers played out, with each finding some happiness and contentment. But the schloss I liked the most was Bückeburg because it has absolutely everything to offer the visitor—beautiful location, fascinating history, and excellent visitor experience.

The Author's Favourite Schlösser

Bückeburg in Lower Saxony
Belvedere in Thuringia
Rheinsberg in Brandenburg
Eutin in Schleswig-Holstein
Burg Stargard in Mecklenburg-Western Pomerania

After two books and fifty schlösser, my appetite for schloss hunting is undiminished. There are still hundreds of beautiful schlösser out there and many more royal families with fascinating stories to tell. In my third book we will return to see more schlösser in beautiful Thuringia, explore Hesse to find out about its royal houses (both Hesse-Darmstadt and Hesse-Kassel), and end at the Rhine where, in the nineteenth century, many ruined schlösser were restored by the Prussian royal family in a romantic image of the past. So watch out for *Schloss III*.

APPENDICES

Appendix A: Map of Germany

The map opposite (which is hand drawn) shows the sixteen federal states of Germany and the approximate location of the twenty-five schlösser included in this book. Please use the list below to match the numbers with the individual schlösser.

1. Bückeburg
2. Oldenburg
3. Rastede Palais
4. Jever
5. Eutin
6. Kiel
7. Wasserschloss Glücksburg
8. Schloss vor Husum
9. Schlossinsel Mirow
10. Hohenzieritz
11. Residenz Neustrelitz
12. Burg Stargard
13. Rheinsberg
14. Saalfeld
15. Friedenstein
16. Reinhardsbrunn
17. Residenzschloss Weimar
18. Belvedere
19. Heidecksburg
20. Schwarzburg
21. Braunschweig
22. Wolfenbüttel
23. Kaiserpfalz Goslar
24. Wolfsburg
25. Fallersleben

Appendix B: List of the Schlösser Included in my Books

Name	Location (if different)	Current use	*Schloss I* or *Schloss II*
Lower Saxony			
Ahlden		Auction house	I
Braunschweig		Museum and shopping centre	II
Bückeburg		Museum	II
Celle		Museum	I
Fallersleben	Wolfsburg	Museum	II
Herrenhausen	Hannover	Gardens open	I
Jever		Museum	II
Kaiserpfalz	Goslar	Museum	II
Marienburg	Pattensen	Museum	I
Oldenburg		Museum	II
Rastede Palais		Museum	II
Little Richmond	Braunschweig	Events venue and park	II
Salzdahlum		Destroyed	II
Stadthagen mausoleum		Mausoleum	II
Wolfenbüttel		Museum	II
Wolfsburg		Museum	II
Schleswig-Holstein			
Blomenburg	Selent	Empty	II
Eutin		Museum	II
Glücksburg		Museum	II
Husum		Museum	II
Kiel		Concert hall	II
Salzau	Fargau-Pratjau	Empty	II

Mecklenburg- Pomerania

Bad Doberan		Government offices	*I*
Blücher	Göhren-Lebbin	Hotel	*II*
Gamehl		Hotel	*I*
Gelbensande		Restaurant and museum	*I*
Güstrow		Museum	*I*
Hohenzieritz		Offices and museum	*II*
Ludwigslust		Museum	*I*
Mirow		Museum	*II*
Neustrelitz		Destroyed	*II*
Schwerin		State Parliament and museum	*I*
Burg Stargard		Museum	*II*
Wiligrad	Lubstorf	Artists' colony	*I*

Berlin and Brandenburg

Altes Palais	Berlin	University	*I*
Cecilienhof	Potsdam	Hotel and museum	*I*
Charlottenburg	Berlin	Museum	*I*
Neues Palais	Potsdam	Museum	*I*
Paretz	Ketzin	Museum	*I*
Rheinsberg		Museum	*II*
Sanssouci	Potsdam	Museum	*I*

Saxony

Burg Stolpen		Museum	*I*
Colditz		Museum	*I*
Pillnitz	Dresden	Museum	*I*
Residenzschloss	Dresden	Museum	*I*
Rochlitz		Museum	*I*
Taschenbergpalais	Dresden	Hotel	*I*

Thuringia

Belvedere	Weimar	Museum	*II*
Friedenstein	Gotha	Museum	*II*
Heidecksburg	Rudolstadt	Museum	*II*
Reinhardsbrunn	Friedrichroda	Empty	*II*
Residenzschloss	Weimar	Museum	*II*
Saalfeld		Government offices	*II*
Schwarzburg		Museum	*II*

Hesse

Bad Homburg		Museum	*I*
Burgruine Königstein		Museum	*I*
Friedrichshof	Kronberg im Taunus	Hotel	*I*
Kronberg		Museum	*I*
Luxembourg	Königstein im Taunus	Law Court	*I*

Rhineland Palatinate

Marksburg	Braubach	German Castles Association and museum	*I*

Appendix C: Timeline from the End of the Thirty Years' War to the Reunification of Germany.

1648. The Peace of Westphalia brings an end to the Thirty Years' War, which had devastated Europe.

1682. Louis XIV of France moves his court into the new palace of Versailles.

1688. Anton Ulrich of Brunswick-Wolfenbüttel starts to build his version of Versailles at Salzdahlum.

1711. Charlotte Christine of Brunswick-Wolfenbüttel marries the son of Peter the Great of Russia.

1714. Elector Georg Ludwig of Hannover becomes King George I of Great Britain.

1726. The last trial for witchcraft in Mecklenburg takes place in Burg Stargard.

1730. Crown Prince Friedrich of Prussia (later Frederick the Great) tries to run away from his father.

1744. Sophie of Anhalt-Zerbst arrives in Russia on approval as a bride for Grand Duke Peter, the heir to the throne.

1756–1763. The Seven Years' War engulfs much of Europe.

1761. Sophie Charlotte of Mecklenburg-Strelitz becomes Queen Charlotte when she marries George III of Great Britain.

1762. Catherine the Great stages a successful coup and becomes the ruler of Russia.

1775. Goethe arrives in Weimar at the invitation of Duke Karl August.

1789. The storming of the Bastille marks the beginning of the French Revolution.

1792. Start of the French Revolutionary Wars.

1803. The process of secularisation and mediatisation of German states begins.

1806. The Holy Roman Empire is dissolved.

1810.	Queen Luise of Prussia dies while visiting her father at Hohenzieritz.
1815.	Napoleon is finally defeated at the Battle of Waterloo. The Congress of Vienna decides the future of the German states.
1820.	The trial of Queen Caroline takes place in the British House of Lords.
1830.	The citizens of Braunschweig overthrow Duke Karl II.
1832.	Prince Otto of Bavaria becomes king of an independent Greece.
1837.	Queen Victoria succeeds to the throne of Great Britain.
1841.	Hoffman von Fallersleben writes 'The Song of Germany', which will later become the German national anthem.
1848.	Start of the First War of Schleswig-Holstein.
1863.	Prince Christian of Glücksburg becomes King Christian IX of Denmark.
1864.	Denmark is defeated in the Second War of Schleswig-Holstein, and the duchies are occupied by Prussia and Austria.
1866.	The Seven Weeks' War; after Austria's defeat, Prussia annexes Schleswig-Holstein.
1871.	Wilhelm I, king of Prussia, is proclaimed emperor (kaiser) of a new German Empire.
1895.	The opening of the Kiel Canal is a major step in the buildup of the German navy.
1901.	The end of an era, as Queen Victoria dies.
1914.	The assassination of Archduke Franz Ferdinand in Sarajevo is the trigger that starts World War I.
1918.	The end of World War I brings revolution in Germany; Kaiser Wilhelm I and the other ruling princes abdicate.
1938.	Hitler lays the foundation stone for a car factory and a new town that will become Wolfsburg.
1939.	World War II begins.
1941.	Ex-kaiser Wilhelm II dies in exile in the Netherlands.

1945.   A defeated Germany is split into four zones of occupation—British, French, US, and Soviet. The Cold War begins.

1949.   Germany becomes two separate countries—the Federal Republic of Germany (West) and the German Democratic Republic (East).

1955.   Beetle number one million rolls off the production line at Wolfsburg.

1961.   The Berlin Wall goes up.

1987.   In a Berlin speech, US president Ronald Reagan challenges Soviet Union leader Mikhail Gorbachev to 'Tear down this Wall!'

1989.   The Berlin Wall comes down.

1990.   Reunification of East and West Germany.

Appendix D: A Brief History of Germany

This appendix gives a brief outline of aspects of German history that are relevant to this book.

The Holy Roman Empire

The Holy Roman Empire of the German Nation was a loose alliance of independent German and central European states under the leadership of an elected emperor. It lasted for over eight hundred years, from the crowning in 962 of the first emperor, Otto the Great, until it was disbanded by the last emperor in 1806. By its name, the empire claimed to be the successor to the Roman empire of the West (which fell to the Barbarians in the fifth century AD), and it was called Holy because early emperors were crowned by the Pope in Rome. However, there is a famous quote by the French philosopher and writer Voltaire that, despite its name, it was 'neither holy, nor Roman, nor an empire.'

The empire extended beyond the boundaries of present-day Germany to include Austria and other Central European states. It comprised hundreds of different pieces of territory that ranged enormously in size from large and powerful states ruled by prince-electors to small principalities centred on a single schloss. As well as the secular states, it included ecclesiastical territories ruled by bishops or archbishops, and a number of free cities.

Within the empire, the member states had self-governing rights, which made it cumbersome and difficult to govern. The states owed allegiance to the emperor, whose role was to keep the peace between members (in which he did not always succeed) and, with their support (which he did not always get), to defend it against external attack. One of the crowning moments in its history was when the imperial armies, under the overall leadership of Emperor Leopold I, defeated the Turks at the Battle of Vienna in 1683 and stopped further encroachment by the Ottoman Empire into Europe.

The Holy Roman emperor was elected by a college of kurfürsten, or prince-electors. There were only a small number of these—for example, in 1692, there were nine. It was an extremely prestigious position with opportunities for lucrative bribes at the time of an election. This was the case even though the position of emperor became a sinecure within the Austrian house of Hapsburg. From the election of the Hapsburg Friedrich III in 1452 to the end of the empire, there was only one non-Hapsburg emperor.

Over the centuries the central powers of the empire were weakened as successive emperors were forced to grant concessions to the member states. But it was the French Revolution and the rise of Napoleon that would eventually bring about its demise. After a number of states left the empire to join a rival grouping under Napoleon's leadership, the last Holy Roman emperor, Francis II, recognised that it had become untenable and dissolved the empire in 1806.

The Impact of Napoleon

The French Revolution and the overthrow of Louis XVI led to a series of wars that lasted for more than twenty years, from 1792, between the new French Republic and the states of the Holy Roman Empire. The original aim of the German states was to overthrow the republic and reinstate the French monarchy. Later however, as Napoleon moved his armies into Germany, the focus shifted to trying to protect their territories against French aggression. By the time Napoleon was finally defeated at the Battle of Waterloo in 1815, the Holy Roman Empire had ceased to exist and the political map of Germany had changed dramatically.

The changes began when, after Napoleon's major victory at the Battle of Marengo, France annexed all of the territory of the German princes to the west of the Rhine. The Holy Roman emperor was forced to agree to compensate them with lands from elsewhere in the empire. Starting in 1803 this process, called secularisation and mediatisation, would have a wide-reaching and lasting effect. At the end of it, the hundreds of pieces of the old Holy Roman Empire had been rationalised and reduced to fewer than fifty.

Under the process of secularisation, virtually all the ecclesiastical territories in the empire were parcelled out among the secular princes. The imperial free cities also lost their independence and were amalgamated into neighbouring territories; only a handful kept their status. And under mediatisation, rulers of the smaller secular states were forced to cede them to the larger.

Napoleon's plan was to create a cluster of French vassal states to the east of the Rhine, and in 1806 he set up the Confederation of the Rhine as a rival grouping to the Holy Roman Empire. This led to the demise of the empire as its member states ceded to join the new confederation. Those who did so were often rewarded by increases in their land or titles; for example, Württemberg and Saxony were promoted to kingdoms.

After France was finally beaten, the Congress of Vienna agreed on the boundaries and the titles for the post-war German states. But major changes had already taken place in the previous years, driven by Napoleon. The impact of Napoleon on the structure of Germany was therefore enormous.

Germany after the Congress of Vienna

At the end of the Napoleonic Wars, the political map of Europe was redrawn in 1815 at the Congress of Vienna. The congress created a new alliance of German and Central European states called the German Confederation. This included Austria, which held the presidency. The German Confederation lasted for fifty years, until it fell apart after the Seven Weeks' War of 1866 when Prussia defeated Austria. This was the end of Austrian influence in Germany, and it left Prussia in the ascendant. Within five years the new German Empire would come into existence with a Prussian emperor.

The German Confederation had forty-one member states, of which thirty-one were ruled by German royal families. The other members were four free cities (Bremen, Frankfurt, Hamburg, and Lübeck), the duchies of Holstein and Lauenburg (which were ruled by the king of · Denmark), and four Central European states that are not part of present-day Germany (Austria, Bohemia, Liechtenstein, and Luxembourg).

The thirty-one German states are listed below.[168] I have used an asterisk* to indicate those whose royal families feature in this book, and another symbol§ to show those featured in my first book on German schlösser (*Schloss I*).

Anhalt-Dessau	Nassau§
Anhalt-Bernburg	Oldenburg*
Anhalt-Köthen	Prussia*§
Baden	Reuss, elder line
Bavaria	Reuss, younger line
Brunswick*	Saxe-Coburg-Saalfeld*
Hannover§	Saxe-Gotha-Altenburg*
Hesse-Darmstadt	Saxe-Hildburghausen
Hesse-Homburg§	Saxe-Meiningen
Hesse-Kassel	Saxe-Weimar-Eisenach*
Hohenzollern-Hechingen	Saxony§
Hohenzollern-Sigmaringen	Schaumberg-Lippe*
Lippe-Detmold	Schwarzburg-Rudolstadt*
Mecklenburg-Schwerin§	Schwarzburg-Sonderhausen
Mecklenburg-Strelitz*	Waldeck-Pyrmont
	Württemberg

The Schleswig-Holstein Question

The disputed duchies of Schleswig and Holstein were the cause of two bitter wars between Denmark and Germany in the mid-nineteenth century.

At the beginning of the nineteenth century, the duchies were ruled by the Danish king but were not part of the kingdom of Denmark proper; they were ruled by the king in a personal union (in the same way that the kings of Great Britain also ruled Hannover between 1714 and 1837). Holstein was actually a state in the Holy Roman Empire and later the German Confederation, while Schleswig was a buffer state between the Confederation and Denmark.

As the century progressed it became increasingly clear that the Danish royal family would die out in the male line, giving rise to issues not only about the succession to the Danish throne but also in Schleswig-Holstein. The Danes wanted to incorporate the duchies as part of Denmark, while many Schleswig-Holsteiners thought they should be combined into an independent state ruled by the duke of Augustenburg. And Prussian Chancellor Bismarck had his own ideas. The narrow Jutland peninsula is bordered by the sea on both sides (the North Sea to the west and the Baltic to the east), and Bismarck particularly coveted the Baltic port of Kiel.

The First War of Schleswig-Holstein lasted between 1848 and 1851, and in Danish history it's usually called the Schleswig-Holstein Rebellion or the Civil War. The peace treaty at the end of the war (the London Protocol of 1852) settled the succession to the throne of Denmark and also confirmed the Danish king's possession of the duchies. However, after Denmark was heavily defeated in the 1864 Second War of Schleswig-Holstein, the two duchies were ceded to the victors, who were Austria and Prussia. After Austria's defeat in the Seven Weeks' War of 1866, they were annexed by Prussia and became the Prussian province of Schleswig-Holstein.

The Unification of Germany (for the First Time)

One legacy of the struggle against Napoleon was a growing movement within Germany for a unified country. Many Germans hoped that the different states would come together as a single nation and develop into a liberal democracy under the leadership of Prussia. The consort of Queen Victoria, Prince Albert, came from Thuringia and shared this vision. He arranged the marriage of his eldest daughter (Vicky) to the Prussian heir to help achieve it (for Vicky's story, see *Schloss I*). But the Prussian takeover of Germany, when it came, would follow a very different model.

In 1861 Vicky's father-in-law, King Wilhelm, succeeded his brother as king of Prussia, and the following year he appointed Bismarck as his chief minister. Over the next ten years, Bismarck would follow what became known as a policy of 'blood and iron' to forge the German Empire.

In 1864 Prussia and Austria defeated Denmark in the Second War of Schleswig-Holstein, and Denmark lost the duchies. Two years later, in 1866, Prussia turned on her previous ally and annexed the two duchies after defeating Austria in the Seven Weeks' War. The German states that had sided with Austria, such as Hannover and Nassau, were also annexed and lost their sovereignty. In another swift campaign in 1870, Prussia defeated France in the Franco-Prussian War, and the French provinces of Alsace and Lorraine were added to Prussian territory. This victory over France, the traditional enemy of Germany, generated the national enthusiasm and pride that led to King Wilhelm being acclaimed as kaiser (or emperor) of a united German empire by the other ruling German princes in the Hall of Mirrors at Versailles Palace near Paris in 1871.

On the formation of the new empire there remained twenty-three German states. Although they retained their own governments and royal families, these had limited sovereignty and power was centralised, with key areas such as defence and foreign affairs being under the control of Prussia.

The German empire did not survive World War I; in November 1918 in the chaos of defeat, Kaiser Wilhelm II (the grandson of the first kaiser) abdicated as German emperor and king of Prussia, followed quickly by the other ruling princes. The ex-kaiser lived the rest of his life in exile in Holland.

SCHLOSS II

Revolution and Republic

By the autumn of 1918 Germany was on the brink of starvation and collapse. The country was demoralised and no one believed any longer that Germany could win the war. When the Baltic Fleet was ordered to sea at the end of October for a last-ditch battle, the sailors rebelled against what they saw as a futile death and mutinied. The revolution spread and within days, the kaiser abdicated, the government resigned, and a republic was declared. Germany capitulated, and an armistice was signed on 11 November.

For a while it hung in the balance as to what sort of system would replace the monarchy. Many on the far left wanted to go down the communist path and follow the model of the Bolshevik revolution in Russia the year before. But the larger and more centrist Social Democratic Party (SDP) favoured an orderly transition to a parliamentary democracy and was prepared to collaborate with the old regime in order to achieve this. Uprisings, such as the Spartacist revolt in Berlin in January 1919, were put down with violence and considerable loss of life.

In February 1919 the members of the newly elected National Assembly (Reichstag) met in Weimar, which had been chosen as a temporary location for the new parliament because of the unrest in Berlin. This is how the town came to give its name to the Weimar Republic. During the nine months it sat in Weimar, the assembly transacted some important business including approving the Versailles Treaty (the peace treaty that ended World War I) and agreeing on the new German constitution, which was signed on 11 August 1919.

But the new republic was under pressure from the start. Tainted by the stigma of defeat and the punitive peace terms imposed by the Allies, it had to face serious economic issues such as hyperinflation, mass unemployment, and the Great Depression. It was also politically unstable, being loathed and attacked from both the left and the right. The left claimed that the workers' revolution had been betrayed; the right perpetuated the myth (which was quite untrue) that the High

204

Command would have won the war if they had not been stabbed in the back by civilians.

Disillusioned by democracy, many Germans turned to the Nazi party, and by 1933 they held nearly half the seats in the Reichstag. President Hindenburg appointed Hitler as the chancellor, and within weeks he had pushed through new legislation that enabled him to rule as a dictator without reference to parliament. This was the end of the Weimar Republic and the beginning of the Third Reich. The following year, after Hindenburg's death, Hitler became the führer.

Germany Divided and Reunified

After the end of World War II in 1945, Germany was divided into four military occupied zones: American, British, French, and Soviet. This division became permanent with the setting up in 1949 of two separate countries, the Federal Republic of Germany (known as West Germany), with its capital in Bonn, and the smaller German Democratic Republic (known as East Germany or the GDR), with its capital in East Berlin. West Germany comprised the old American, British, and French zones and was a parliamentary democracy with a capitalist economy. The GDR (previously the Soviet zone) was communist and part of the Soviet bloc. This period when Germany was split between East and West in the Cold War is known as the division of Germany.

The defeat and dismemberment of Germany caused enormous suffering and displaced millions of Germans from their homes. In her memoirs, Duchess Viktoria Luise of Brunswick (the only daughter of Kaiser Wilhelm II) wrote about trying to help the great influx of German refugees who had been expelled from the Eastern bloc, and how she stood on the border with Chancellor Konrad Adenauer in 1954 to greet returning prisoners of war from Russian camps.[169] She herself had been a refugee fleeing from the Soviet army in 1945.

In the 1950s the West German economy began to grow at a fast rate (called the *economic miracle*), and it would become the most prosperous country in Europe. Under the Soviet system the economy of the GDR stagnated, and living standards were much lower. To prevent the mass migration of its citizens, East Germany closed its border in 1961 so that an 'iron curtain' was in place against the West. Its most potent symbol was the Berlin Wall, which ran through some of the most historic parts of the city, notably the Brandenburg Gate.

By 1989 the Soviet Union had loosened its hold on the Eastern Bloc countries. The crumbling East German regime could not resist the trend toward greater freedom for its citizens and, on 9 November 1989, the crossing points in the Berlin Wall were opened. Thousands of East Berliners streamed through to be greeted by cheering Westerners; it was a highly emotional night. Within days the wall was being demolished. After the entire East German government resigned the first free elections were held, and negotiations with the West began. After forty-five years apart, Germany was reunited on 3 October 1990, when the GDR became part of the Federal Republic of Germany.

Germany Today

The Federal Republic of Germany is a parliamentary democracy with two levels of elected government—the Bundestag, which is the federal parliament in Berlin, and the Bundesrat, which are the parliaments of Germany's regional states.

The republic is made up of sixteen regional states, or länder. On reunification in 1990, the ten existing states of Western Germany were joined by five reconstituted states from Eastern Germany. The sixteenth is the city of Berlin.

Many of these states retain the names of the old kingdoms and principalities that were their forerunners; for example, Baden-Württemberg, Bavaria, Saxony, and Brandenburg. Notable by its absence however is the name of Prussia. After World War II the victorious Allies, being determined not to see a resurgence of Prussian militaristic values, passed a law that the state of Prussia should never again exist.

Appendix E: Charts and Family Trees

1. Some counts and princes of Schaumburg-Lippe who left their mark on Schloss Bückeburg.
2. The family tree of Duke Peter Friedrich Ludwig of Oldenburg (PFL).
3. The House of Oldenburg showing the branches included in this book.
4. The close links between the Holstein-Gottorf family and the tsars of Russia.
5. The claims of Karl Peter Ulrich of Holstein-Gottorf to the thrones of both Sweden and Russia.
6. The extraordinary interconnection of Europe's royal families on the outbreak of war in 1914.
7. How Christian IX succeeded to the Danish throne.
8. The family relationship between three princesses associated with Mecklenburg-Strelitz.
9. The eight dukes of Mecklenburg-Strelitz.
10. Frederick the Great and his siblings.
11. The history of the duchy of Saxe-Saalfeld and how it became Saxe-Coburg-Gotha.
12. The descent of Prince George of Cambridge from the dukes of Saxe-Saalfeld.
13. A family tree for the dukes of Saxe-Weimar-Eisenach.
14. How the princes of Schwarzburg-Rudolstadt ran out of sons.
15. The Brunswick-Wolfenbüttel family: a tradition of great soldiers and of princesses who married emperors and kings.

1. SOME COUNTS AND PRINCES OF SCHAUMBURG-LIPPE WHO LEFT THEIR MARK ON SCHLOSS BÜCKEBURG

Holstein - Schaumburg

Schaumburg - Lippe

Otto IV
1517 - 1576
*Converted the small castle
at Bückeburg
into a four-winged palace*

Philipp
1601 - 1681
*A distant cousin became the first count
when the new state was created
in 1647*

Ernst
1569 - 1622
*Otto's son transformed Bückeburg into a
sophisticated Renaissance Court and
built the wonderful mausoleum at
Stadthagen.
He was made a prince of the Holy
Roman Empire*

Wilhelm
1724 - 1777
*Philipp's great grandson was born and
brought up in England. He was a famous
military commander who fortified the
state. He had no children and was
succeeded by his cousin, Philipp Ernst*

Georg Wilhelm
1784 - 1860
*The son of Philipp Ernst, he was two when
his father died. He reigned for 73 years,
becoming a prince in 1807. He was a good
businessman who built up a large fortune*

*Ernst left no children and
the line died out in the 1640s*

Adolf Georg
1817 - 1893
*The son of Georg Wilhelm, he sided with
Prussia in the 1860s and as a result kept
his principality independent*

Georg
1846 – 1911
*He was the son of Adolf Georg and built
the right wing and Cavalier houses at
Bückeburg to create a grand new entrance*

Holstein-Schaumburg was the previous
name of the Schaumburg-Lippe family

——— solid lines show a
father/son relationship

- - - - - - broken lines show a
more indirect family relationship

Adolf II
1883 – 1936
*Georg's son, he built the mausoleum and
was the last reigning prince*

2. THE FAMILY TREE OF DUKE PETER FRIEDRICH LUDWIG OF OLDENBURG (PFL)

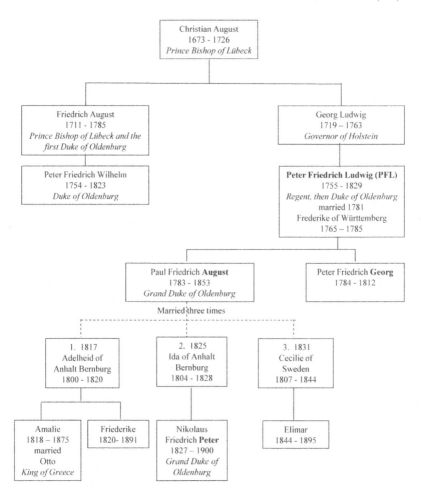

Christian August
1673 - 1726
Prince Bishop of Lübeck

Friedrich August
1711 - 1785
*Prince Bishop of Lübeck and the
first Duke of Oldenburg*

Georg Ludwig
1719 – 1763
Governor of Holstein

Peter Friedrich Wilhelm
1754 - 1823
Duke of Oldenburg

Peter Friedrich Ludwig (PFL)
1755 - 1829
Regent, then Duke of Oldenburg
married 1781
Frederike of Württemberg
1765 – 1785

Paul Friedrich **August**
1783 - 1853
Grand Duke of Oldenburg

Peter Friedrich **Georg**
1784 - 1812

Married three times

1. 1817
Adelheid of
Anhalt Bernburg
1800 - 1820

2. 1825
Ida of Anhalt
Bernburg
1804 - 1828

3. 1831
Cecilie of
Sweden
1807 - 1844

Amalie
1818 – 1875
married
Otto
King of Greece

Friederike
1820- 1891

Nikolaus
Friedrich **Peter**
1827 – 1900
*Grand Duke of
Oldenburg*

Elimar
1844 - 1895

3. THE HOUSE OF OLDENBURG SHOWING THE BRANCHES
INCLUDED IN THIS BOOK

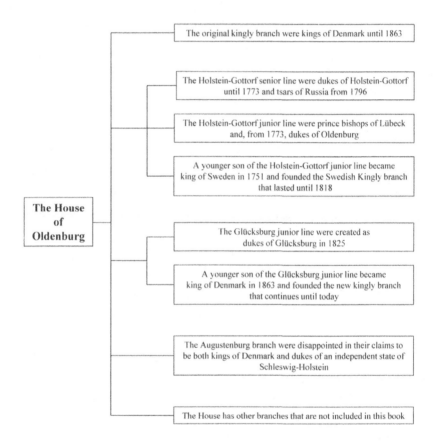

The House of Oldenburg

- The original kingly branch were kings of Denmark until 1863

- The Holstein-Gottorf senior line were dukes of Holstein-Gottorf until 1773 and tsars of Russia from 1796

- The Holstein-Gottorf junior line were prince bishops of Lübeck and, from 1773, dukes of Oldenburg

- A younger son of the Holstein-Gottorf junior line became king of Sweden in 1751 and founded the Swedish Kingly branch that lasted until 1818

- The Glücksburg junior line were created as dukes of Glücksburg in 1825

- A younger son of the Glücksburg junior line became king of Denmark in 1863 and founded the new kingly branch that continues until today

- The Augustenburg branch were disappointed in their claims to be both kings of Denmark and dukes of an independent state of Schleswig-Holstein

- The House has other branches that are not included in this book

**4. THE CLOSE LINKS BETWEEN THE HOLSTEIN-GOTTORF FAMILY AND
THE TSARS OF RUSSIA**

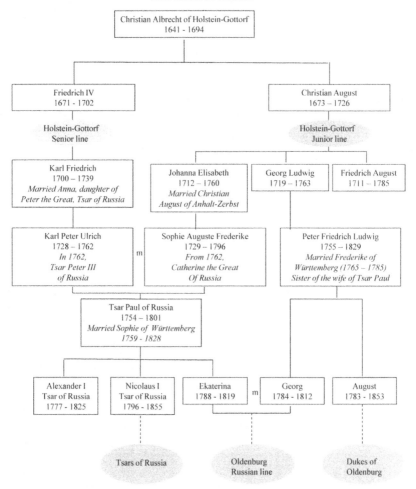

5. THE CLAIMS OF KARL PETER ULRICH OF HOLSTEIN-GOTTORF
TO THE THRONES OF BOTH SWEDEN & RUSSIA

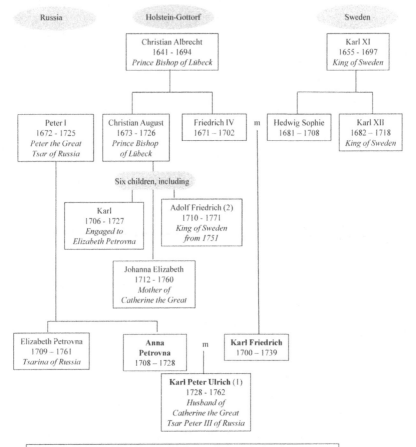

(1) Peter was tsar of Russia for a few months in 1762. He was succeeded by his wife,
Catherine the Great, and on her death in 1796 by their son, Paul.

(2) When Peter became heir to the Russian throne in 1742, his claim to the Swedish throne
was taken over by a relative, Adolf Friedrich, who became King of Sweden in 1751.

6. THE EXTRAORDINARY INTERCONNECTION OF EUROPE'S ROYAL FAMILIES ON THE OUTBREAK OF WAR IN 1914

The sovereigns to whom Henry & Irene of Prussia were closely related

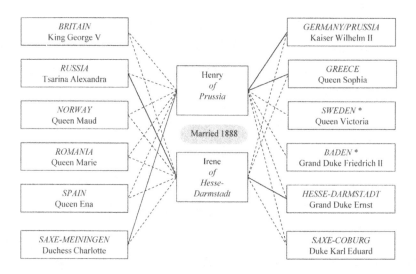

The chart shows the kings or queens of European countries, and rulers of the German states, who were a sibling or first cousin of Henry or Irene, or both.

——————— Sibling (brother or sister)

- - - - - - - - First cousin

* Apart from the two indicated with an asterisk, all the royals shown on this chart were grandchildren of Queen Victoria of Great Britain.

7. HOW CHRISTIAN IX SUCCEEDED TO THE DANISH THRONE

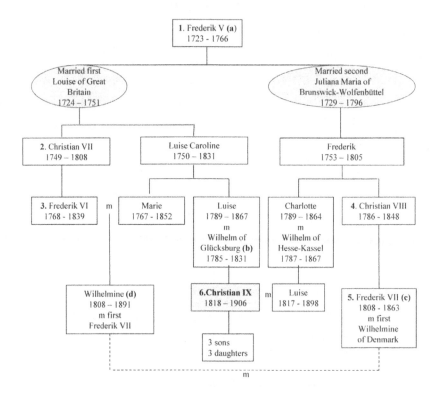

The numbers 1 – 6 show the order of succession of Danish Kings, starting with Frederik V

(a) Frederik V married twice and had a son by each of his wives.

(b) Wilhelm was created duke of Glücksburg in 1825 by his wife's brother-in-law, Frederik VI .

(c) Frederik VII made two dynastic marriages, both of which ended in divorce. His third marriage was morganatic. There were no children by any of his three marriages.

(d) Wilhelmine's second marriage was to Karl of Glücksburg (the elder brother of Christian IX)). There were no children by either marriage.

8. THE FAMILY RELATIONSHIP BETWEEN THREE PRINCESSES ASSOCIATED WITH MECKLENBURG-STRELITZ

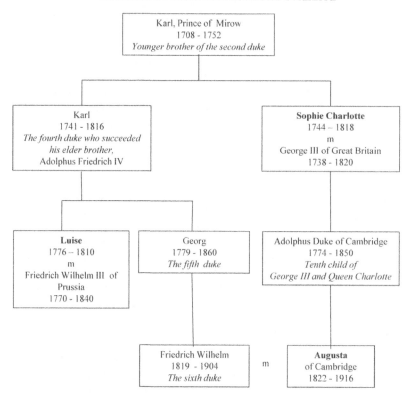

9. THE EIGHT DUKES OF MECKLENBURG-STRELITZ

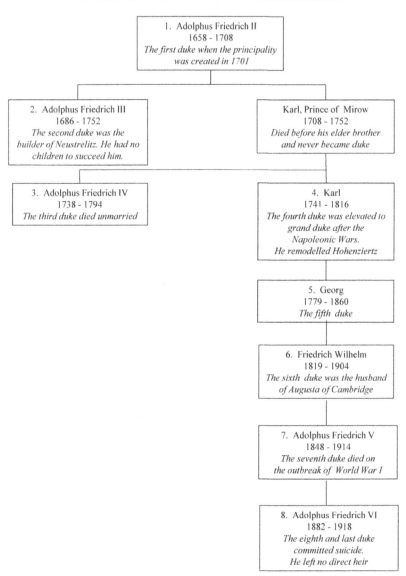

> 1. Adolphus Friedrich II
> 1658 - 1708
> *The first duke when the principality
> was created in 1701*

> 2. Adolphus Friedrich III
> 1686 - 1752
> *The second duke was the
> builder of Neustrelitz. He had no
> children to succeed him.*

> Karl, Prince of Mirow
> 1708 - 1752
> *Died before his elder brother
> and never became duke*

> 3. Adolphus Friedrich IV
> 1738 - 1794
> *The third duke died unmarried*

> 4. Karl
> 1741 - 1816
> *The fourth duke was elevated to
> grand duke after the
> Napoleonic Wars.
> He remodelled Hohenziertz*

> 5. Georg
> 1779 - 1860
> *The fifth duke*

> 6. Friedrich Wilhelm
> 1819 - 1904
> *The sixth duke was the husband
> of Augusta of Cambridge*

> 7. Adolphus Friedrich V
> 1848 - 1914
> *The seventh duke died on
> the outbreak of World War I*

> 8. Adolphus Friedrich VI
> 1882 - 1918
> *The eighth and last duke
> committed suicide.
> He left no direct heir*

216

10. FREDERICK THE GREAT AND HIS SIBLINGS

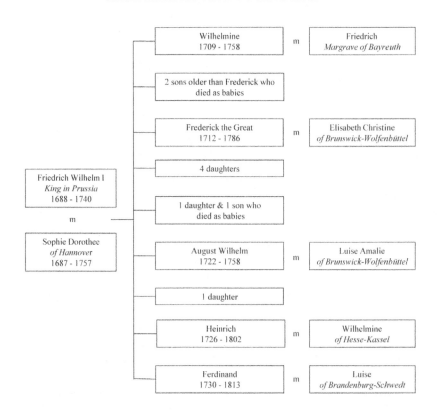

1. Between 1707 and 1730, Friederich Wilhelm I and his wife had 14 children, of whom four (three boys and a girl) did not survive babyhood.
2. When Frederick the Great died in 1786, he was succeeded by the son of August Wilhelm, who became Friedrich Wilhelm II.
3. The wives of Frederick the Great and August Wilhelm were sisters.

11. THE HISTORY OF THE DUCHY OF SAXE-SAALFELD AND HOW IT BECAME SAXE-COBURG-GOTHA

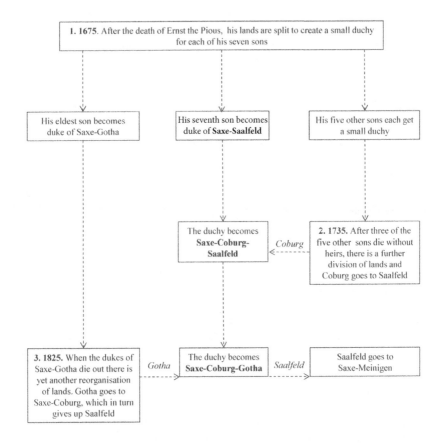

12. THE DESCENT OF PRINCE GEORGE OF CAMBRIDGE FROM THE DUKES OF SAXE-SAALFELD

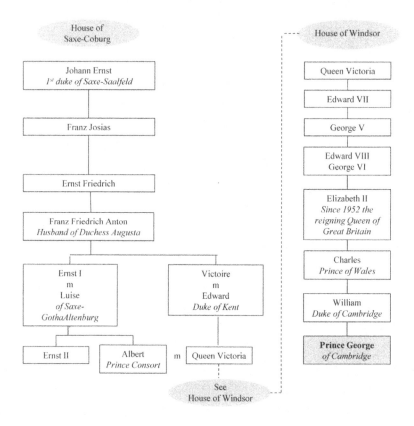

---

1. This chart covers 13 generations from the birth of Johann Ernst, 1st duke of Saxe-Saalfeld, in 1658 to the birth of Prince George of Cambridge in 2013. Prince George is the 10 times great grandson of Johann Ernst.
2. From 1840, when Queen Victoria married Prince Albert, the surname of the British royal family was Saxe-Coburg-Gotha. This was until World War I (1917) when George V changed it to Windsor, for fear of being thought too German.
3. Edward VIII and George VI were brothers. Queen Elizabeth is the daughter of the younger brother, George VI.

13. A FAMILY TREE FOR THE DUKES OF SAXE-WEIMAR-EISENACH

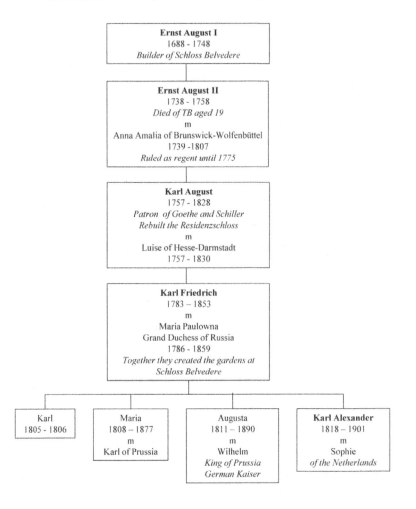

Ernst August I
1688 - 1748
Builder of Schloss Belvedere

Ernst August II
1738 - 1758
Died of TB aged 19
m
Anna Amalia of Brunswick-Wolfenbüttel
1739 -1807
Ruled as regent until 1775

Karl August
1757 - 1828
Patron of Goethe and Schiller
Rebuilt the Residenzschloss
m
Luise of Hesse-Darmstadt
1757 - 1830

Karl Friedrich
1783 – 1853
m
Maria Paulowna
Grand Duchess of Russia
1786 - 1859
Together they created the gardens at
Schloss Belvedere

Karl	Maria	Augusta	**Karl Alexander**
1805 - 1806	1808 – 1877	1811 – 1890	1818 – 1901
	m	m	m
	Karl of Prussia	Wilhelm	Sophie
		King of Prussia	*of the Netherlands*
		German Kaiser	

1. From 1741 the duchies of Saxe-Weimar and Saxe-Eisenach were ruled by the duke in a personal union. In 1809 the two duchies were merged.
2. Karl August was promoted from Duke to Grand Duke at the Congress of Vienna in 1815.

14. HOW THE PRINCES OF SCHWARZBURG-RUDOLSTADT RAN OUT OF SONS

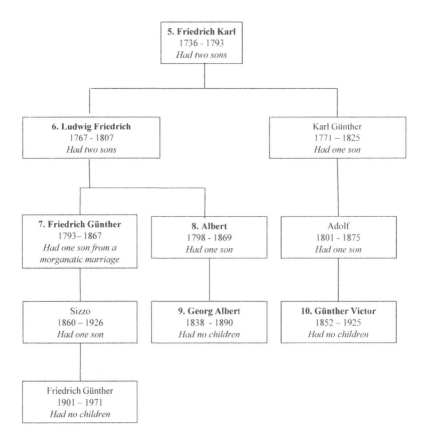

5. Friedrich Karl
1736 - 1793
Had two sons

6. Ludwig Friedrich
1767 - 1807
Had two sons

Karl Günther
1771 – 1825
Had one son

7. Friedrich Günther
1793– 1867
Had one son from a morganatic marriage

8. Albert
1798 - 1869
Had one son

Adolf
1801 - 1875
Had one son

Sizzo
1860 – 1926
Had one son

9. Georg Albert
1838 - 1890
Had no children

10. Günther Victor
1852 – 1925
Had no children

Friedrich Günther
1901 – 1971
Had no children

This chart shows (in bold) the last six of the 10 reigning princes and indicates the order in which they reigned. It includes only those sons who survived childhood.

15. THE BRUNSWICK-WOLFENBÜTTEL FAMILY
A TRADITION OF GREAT SOLDIERS AND OF PRINCESSES
WHO MARRIED EMPERORS AND KINGS

Parents	Children		
Ludwig Rudolf (Son of Anton Ulrich) m Christine Luise *of Oettingen*	Elizabeth Christine 1691 - 1750 m Karl VI *Holy Roman Emperor*	Charlotte Christine Sophie 1694 - 1715 m Alexei *Tsarevich of Russia*	Antoinette Amalie 1696 - 1762 m Ferdinand Albrecht II *Duke of Brunswick-Wolfenbüttel*
Ferdinand Albrecht II m Antoinette Amalie	Karl I 1713 - 1780 m Philippine Charlotte *of Prussia*	Elizabeth Christine 1715 - 1797 m Frederick the Great *of Prussia*	Ferdinand 1721 – 1792 *Prussian Field Marshal* / Juliana Maria 1729 – 1796 m Friedrich V *of Denmark*
Karl I m Philippine Charlotte	Karl Wilhelm Ferdinand 1735 - 1806 *Prussian Field Marshal* m Augusta *of Great Britain*	Elizabeth Christine Ulrike 1746 - 1840 m Friedrich Wilhelm II *King of Prussia*	Anna Amalia 1739 - 1807 m Ernst August II *Duke of Saxe-Weimar*
Karl Wilhelm Ferdinand m Augusta	Augusta 1764 - 1788 m Friedrich I *King of Württemberg*	Caroline 1768 - 1821 m George IV *of Great Britain*	Friedrich Wilhelm 1771 – 1815 *The Black Duke* m Marie *of Baden*

This chart shows four generations and the dotted lines indicate descent to the next generation.

Appendix F: List of Illustrations

Unless otherwise credited, illustrations are from the author's collection.

1. Bückeburg is a special place—a treasure house of history and art.
2. The Schaumberg-Lippe were a talented family—on the left Graf Wilhelm, who was the military genius of the family; on the right Prince Georg Wilhelm, a good businessman who built up the family fortunes (courtesy of Schloss Bückeburg).
3. The opulent Festival Hall at Schloss Bückeburg (courtesy of Schloss Bückeburg).
4. Schloss Oldenburg is a grand baroque building, painted in soft pale yellow with interesting carved stone detailing (courtesy of Niedersächsische Landesmuseen Oldenburg).
5. Duke Peter Friedrich Ludwig of Oldenburg is always affectionately known as PFL (courtesy of Niedersächsische Landesmuseen Oldenburg).
6. Rastede Palais was the much-loved childhood summer home of Amalie of Oldenburg, later queen of Greece (courtesy of Rastede Palais).
7. Amalie has been called the princess with three mothers, because all of her father's three wives died young as a result of childbirth (courtesy of Rastede Palais).
8. King Otto and Queen Amalie wearing Greek costume in the cathedral at Athens; they never achieved much popularity among their subjects.
9. A central tower, sixty-seven metres tall, dwarfs the front of the schloss at Jever.
10. Catherine the Great was born the princess of an insignificant German duchy, but used her body and her brains to become ruler of the vast Russian empire.
11. A plaque commemorates events at Schloss Jever on 3 May 1945, at the end of World War II.
12. Schloss Eutin is a stunning building set in a beautiful area known as Holstein's Switzerland.
13. Eutin is set against a backdrop of greenery and water.
14. The old schloss at Kiel was destroyed by bombs in 1944; the present building dates from the 1960s and is a concert hall.
15. Prince Henry of Prussia and his wife Irene pictured at the time of their marriage.

16. The wasserschloss (or water castle) at Glücksburg truly deserves its name; the foundations rise directly out of the lake on three sides.
17. A romantic view of Glücksburg in an old picture, with swans on the lake.
18. Alexandra, the beautiful eldest daughter of Prince Christian of Glücksburg, married the Prince of Wales in the same year that her father became the king of Denmark and her brother the king of Greece.
19. Schloss vor Husum is built of brick in the Dutch Renaissance style, with interspersed horizontal courses of cream-coloured sandstone (courtesy of Dr Ulf von Hielmcrone).
20. The main door at Husum with brick arch and coat of arms.
21. The elaborate carved stone fireplaces at Husum were saved on the orders of the king of Denmark (courtesy of Dr Ulf von Hielmcrone/Susan Symons).
22. Mirow in the Mecklenburg Lake District was built for the widow of the first duke of Mecklenburg-Strelitz.
23. Princess Sophie Charlotte of Mecklenburg-Strelitz was picked from a list to marry the king of England.
24. The Lower Palace where Queen Charlotte lived as a child has not been restored and looked sad and neglected.
25. Hohenzieritz was the summer home of Grand Duke Karl of Mecklenburg-Strelitz.
26. The room at Hohenzieritz where Queen Luise of Prussia died (aged only thirty-four) is now a fascinating small museum (courtesy of KLG Schloss Hohenzieritz).
27. The grand palace at Neustrelitz was built in imitation of Versailles.
28. The site of the palace is still a beautiful spot; view from the lake up through the gardens to where Schloss Neustrelitz once stood.
29. Burg Stargard is a fine example of the Brick Gothic style of architecture, which is found around the Baltic Sea.
30. Burg Stargard is the oldest secular building in Mecklenburg (courtesy of Burg Stargard/Katja Enthaler).
31. The rustic café in the barn at Burg Stargard was our favourite of the tour (courtesy of Burg Stargard/Katja Enthaler).
32. Schloss Rheinsberg was the home where Frederick the Great of Prussia and later his younger brother, Prince Heinrich, found happiness and contentment.
33. Statue of Frederick the Great outside the gates at Rheinsberg.
34. Frederick the Great as crown prince with his three younger brothers; Heinrich is on the right.

35. The schloss at Saalfeld was built by the ancestor of Prince George of Cambridge (courtesy of Schloss Saalfeld/Peter Lahann).
36. In her diary, Duchess Augusta of Saxe-Coburg described how she watched the Battle of Saalfeld from the schloss windows (courtesy of Stadtmuseum Saalfeld im Franziskanerkloster).
37. Prince Luis Ferdinand was killed in hand-to-hand fighting at Saalfeld.
38. Friedenstein was the first castle to be built after the Thirty Years' War, and its name means Rock of Peace.
39. When Duke Ernst the Pious died his duchy was divided between his seven sons.
40. Prince Albert was the second son of Duchess Luise.
41. Schloss Reinhardsbrunn was built by Duke Ernst I of Saxe-Coburg in fashionable Gothic Revival style (courtesy of Joachim Ortlepp).
42. In its heyday, Reinhardsbrunn played host to much of Europe's royal circle (courtesy of Joachim Ortlepp).
43. Queen Victoria was a relatively new widow when she stayed at Reinhardsbrunn in 1862.
44. Goethe and Schiller lived in Weimar during its golden age; the statue of the two men outside the theatre is said to be the most famous in Germany (courtesy of Philip Bird LRPS CPAGB/Shutterstock.com).
45. The neoclassical Residenzschloss at Weimar (right) is a great contrast in style to the old baroque schloss it replaced (left).
46. Belvedere is a jewel that fits perfectly into its sylvan surroundings.
47. Schloss Heidecksburg where, in the decoration of the rococo rooms, make-believe figures gambol through an imaginary landscape.
48. The natural beauty of the site of Schloss Schwarzburg is unsurpassed.
49. Schwarzburg was gutted by the Nazis and left an uninhabitable ruin (courtesy of Bearn Bilker).
50. The life of Anna Luise spanned a period of extraordinary upheaval (courtesy of the Thuringian State Museum Heidecksburg Rudolstadt).
51. Schloss Braunschweig was destroyed in World War II but rebuilt and opened as a shopping centre in 2007.
52. Karl Wilhelm Ferdinand of Brunswick-Wolfenbüttel was the greatest soldier of his age.
53. Caroline of Brunswick arrives in Britain in 1795 to marry the prince of Wales.

54. The grand entrance at Wolfenbüttel is across the bridge and through a triumphal arch; the little boat in the moat was part of a travelling funfair.

55. The Little Palace at Wolfenbüttel was once the residence of the hereditary crown prince.

56. Kaiserpfalz Goslar was one of more than one hundred imperial palaces used by the Holy Roman emperors.

57. Kaiser Wilhelm I and his son, Crown Prince Friedrich, visited Goslar in 1875.

58. Emperor Friedrich Barbarossa stands guard outside Goslar.

59. Each padlock on the chain at Wolfsburg commemorates a wedding that took place there.

60. At Fallersleben there was a brand-new exhibition about the German National Anthem.

61. The band was playing and a choir singing on the green at Fallersleben.

Bibliography

Ahrendt, Dorothee. *Belvedere Palace Park*. Weimar: Klassik Stiftung Weimar, 2009.

Ashdown, Dulcie M. *Victoria and the Coburgs*. London: Robert Hale, 1981.

Augusta, Duchess of Saxe-Coburg-Saalfeld. *In Napoleonic Days: Extracts from the Private Diary of Augusta, Duchess of Saxe-Coburg-Saalfeld, Queen Victoria's maternal grandmother, 1806–1821: Selected and Translated by H.R.H. The Princess Beatrice*. London: John Murray, 1941.

Bearn, Bilker. 'Princess Elisabeth-Caroline zu Solms-Braunfels, 1916–2013'. *Royalty Digest Quarterly 3* (2013).

Beéche, Arturo E. *The Coburgs of Europe: The Rise and Fall of Queen Victoria and Prince Albert's European Family*. East Richmond Heights: Eurohistory.com, 2014.

Beéche, Arturo E. and Coryne Hall. *Apapa: King Christian IX of Denmark and His Descendants*. East Richmond Heights: Eurohistory.com, 2014.

Bower, Leonard and Gordon Bolitho. *Otho I: King of Greece, A Biography*. London: Selwyn and Blount Ltd, 1939. Reprinted by *Royalty Digest* 2001.

Cavaliero, Roderick. *Genius, Power and Magic: A Cultural History of Germany from Goethe to Wagner*. London: I.B. Taurus, 2013.

Clark, Christopher. *Iron Kingdom: The Rise and Downfall of Prussia 1600–1947*. London: Penguin Books, 2007.

Cruse, Mark and Hilde Hoogenboom. *The Memoirs of Catherine The Great: A New Translation by Mark Cruse and Hilde Hoogenboom*. New York: Modern Library, 2006.

Davison, Anne. *Holy Roman Empire: Power Politics Papacy*. In Brief: Books for Busy People, 2014.

Drinkuth, Friederike. *Queen Charlotte: A Princess from Mecklenburg-Strelitz Ascends the Throne of England*. Schwerin: Thomas Helms Verlag, 2011.

Duff, David. *Hessian Tapestry*. London: Frederick Muller, 1967.

Duggan, J. N. *Sophia of Hanover: From Winter Princess to Heiress of Great Britain, 1630–1714*. London: Peter Owens Publishers, 2010.

Easum, Chester V. *Prince Henry of Prussia: Brother of Frederick the Great*. Wisconsin: The University of Wisconsin Press, 1942.

Fitzmaurice, Lord Edmond. *Charles William Ferdinand, Duke of Brunswick: An Historical Study, 1735–1806*. London: Longmans Green and Co, 1901.

Fleischer, Horst, Frank Esche, Lutz Unbehaun, Doreen Winker, Eberhard Mey, and Jens Henkel. *Die Fürsten von Schwarzburg-Rudolstadt: 1710–1918*. Thüringer Landesmuseum Heidecksburg Rudolstadt, 2001.

Fraser, David. *Frederick the Great: King of Prussia*. London: Allen Lane, Penguin Press, 2000.

Fraser, Flora. *The Unruly Queen: The Life of Queen Caroline*. London: Macmillan, 1996.

Gehrlein, Thomas. *Das Haus Mecklenburg*. Werl: Borde Verlag, 2012.

Gerard, Frances. *A Grand Duchess: The Life of Anna Amalia Duchess of Saxe-Weimar-Eisenach and the Classical Circle of Weimar*. London: Hutchinson & Co, 1902.

Gerlinde Gräfin von Westphalen, *Anna Luise von Schwarzburg: Die Letzte Fürstin*. Jena: Jenzig-Verlag Gabriele Köhler, 2011.

Gold, Claudia. *The King's Mistress: The True and Scandalous Story of The Woman Who Stole the Heart of George I*. London: Quercus, 2012.

Grote, Hans-Henning. *Wolfenbüttel Palace: Residence of the Dukes of Brunswick and Lüneburg*. Braunschweig: Appelhans, 2008.

Hedley, Olwen. *Queen Charlotte*. London: John Murray, 1975.

Hibbert, Christopher, ed. *Queen Victoria in Her Letters and Journals: A Selection by Christopher Hibbert*. New York: Viking, 1985.

Hibbert, Christopher, ed. *Memoirs of the Public and Private Life of Queen Caroline by Joseph Nightingale (1820)*. London: The Folio Society, 1978.

Jung, Ursula. *Goslar: Free Imperial City at the Hartz*. Lübeck: Schoning Verlag.

Klein, Sven Michael. *Das Haus Sachsen-Weimar-Eisenach*. Werl: Borde Verlag, 2013.

Kroll, Maria. *Sophie: Electress of Hanover: A Personal Portrait*. London: Victor Gollancz Ltd, 1973.

Lalor, William Mead. 'The Daughters of Tsar Paul I'. *The Grand Duchesses: Daughters and Granddaughters of Russia's Tsars*. Edited by Arturo E. Beéche. Oakland: Eurohistory.Com, 2004.

Lerche, Anna and Marcus Mandal. *A Royal Family: The Story of Christian IX and his European Descendants*. Copenhagen: Egmont Lademann A/S/Aschehoug, 2003.

Levey, Michael. *A Royal Subject: Portraits of Queen Charlotte*. London: The National Gallery, 1977.

Louda, Jiří and Michael Maclagan. *Lines of Succession: Heraldry of the Royal Families of Europe*. London: Orbis Publishing, 1981.

Lovell, Mary S. *A Scandalous Life: The Biography of Jane Digby el Mezrab*. London: Richard Cohen Books, 1995.

Luise-Sophie, Princess Friedrich Leopold of Prussia. *Behind the Scenes at The Prussian Court*. London: John Murray, 1939.

Massie, Robert K. *Catherine The Great: Portrait of a Woman*. London: Head of Zeus Ltd, 2013.

Mateos Sainz de Medrano, Ricardo. 'L'Affaire Jametel'. *Royalty Digest: A Journal of Record*. 1999.

McIntosh, David. *The Grand Dukes of Oldenburg.* Falköping: Rosvall Royal Books, 2007.

Merten, Klaus. *German Castles and Palaces.* London: Thames and Hudson, 1999.

Moser, Juliane and Stiasy, Tomke. *Eutin Castle.* Berlin: Deutscher Kunstverlag, 2010.

Müller, Wolfgang J. *Glücksburg Castle.* Glücksburg: Siftung Schloss Glücksburg.

Murken, Jan. *Griechenland aus erster Hand: Königin Amalie berichtet ihrem Vater.* Schriftenreihe des Otto Konig museums der Gemeinde Ottobrun, Nr14, 2013.

Nelson, Walter Henry. *The Soldier Kings: The House of Hohenzollern.* Lonson: J. M. Dent & Sons Ltd, 1971.

Pawlow, Kamen. *Gotha, a City Worth Visiting: Travel Guide Including Useful Information about Art, Nature and Sport.* Kamen Pawlow, 2008.

Perl, Alexander and Susan Layton-O'Sullivan. *Schloss Bückeburg: Official Guide.* Hamburg: Discover Guides.

Pope-Hennessy, James. *Queen Mary.* London: Phoenix Press, 2000.

Ridley, Jane. *Bertie: A Life of Edward VII.* London: Chatto and Windus, 2012.

Rounding, Virginia. *Catherine the Great: Love, Sex and Power.* London: Hutchinson, 2006.

Schnaibel, Marlies. *Luise: Queen of Prussia.* Karwe: Edition Rieger, 2005.

Schencks Castles and Gardens: Historic Houses and Heritage Sights. Hamburg: Schenck Verlag, 2012.

Schultz, Hans Adolf. Burgen, Schlösser und Herrensitze im Raum Gifhorn-Wolfsburg. *Schriftenreihe zur Heimatkunde der Sparkasse Gifhorn-Wolfsburg, Band I.*

Seifert, Rita. *Weimar: European Cultural Centre, Cradle of German Classicism*, 3rd ed. Lübeck: Schoning Verlag.

Siems, Maren. *The Princely Gallery in Jever Castle.* Schlossmuseum Jever, 2005.

Sommer, Claudia and Detlef Fuchs. *Rheinsberg Palace.* Berlin: Stiftung Preussische Schlösser und Gärten Berlin-Brandenburg, Deutscher Kunstverlag, 2009.

Sotnick, Richard. *The Coburg Conspiracy: Victoria and Albert—Royal Plots and Manoeuvres.* Great Britain: Ephesus Publishing, 2010.

Time to Travel: Travel in Time to Germany's Finest Stately Homes, Gardens, Castles, and Abbeys. Regensburg: Schnell and Steiner, 2010.

Ulferts, Gert-Dieter. *Belvedere Palace.* Weimar: Klassik Stiftung Weimar, 2009.

Van der Kiste, John. 'Prince Henry of Prussia'. *Royalty Digest: A Journal of Record* (Volume II, no 8, February 1993).

Victoria, Queen of Great Britain and Ireland. *Queen Victoria's Journals.* www. queenvictoriasjournals.org.

Watkins, John. *Memoirs of Her Most Excellent Majesty Sophia-Charlotte, Queen of Great Britain, From Authentic Documents.* London: Henry Colburn, 1819.

Welp, Jörgen, ed. *Dem Wohle Oldenburgs gewidmet: Aspekte kulturellen und sozialen Wirkens des Hauses Oldenburg 1773–1918.* Oldenburg: Isensee Verlag, 2004.

Wilhelmina, Margravine of Bayreuth. *The Misfortunate Margravine: Early memoirs of Wilhelmina, Margravine of Bayreuth, Sister of Frederick the Great; With a Foreword by Pamela Hansford Johnson.* London: Macmillan and Co Ltd, 1970.

Woodham-Smith, Cecil. *Queen Victoria: Her Life and Times, 1819–1861.* London: Hamish Hamilton, 1972.

Wright, Constance. *Louise, Queen of Prussia: A Biography.* London: Frederick Muller, 1970.

Zeepvat, Charlotte. Schleswig-Holstein: 'A Family Album'. *Royalty Digest Quarterly.* 4 (2007).

Zeepvat, Charlotte. The Last Grand Duke: Adolf Friedrich VI of Mecklenburg-Strelitz'. *Royalty Digest Quarterly.* 1 (2008).

Zeepvat, Charlotte. Schwarzburg-Rudolstadt: A Family Album'. *Royalty Digest Quarterly.* 2 (2014).

Zeune, Joachim. *Castles and Palaces: Germany.* Regensburg: Schmidt Verlag, 2004.

Zschokke, Heinrich. *The Princess of Brunswick-Wolfenbüttel and Other Tales: Collection of German Authors, Volume 8.* Leipzig: Bernhard Tauchnitz, 1867.

Notes

Chapter 1
1. Susan Symons, *Schloss: The Fascinating Royal History of 25 German Castles* (Truro: Roseland Books, 2014).

Chapter 2
2. Klaus Merten, *German Castles and Palaces* (London: Thames and Hudson, 1999), 106.
3. Jonathan Petropoulos, *Royals and the Reich: The Princes von Hessen in Nazi Germany* (New York: Oxford University Press, 2006), 58.
4. Alexander Perl and Susan Layton-O'Sullivan, *Schloss Bückeburg: Official Guide* (Hamburg: Discover Guides), 53.
5. J. N. Duggan, *Sophia of Hanover: From Winter Princess to Heiress of Great Britain, 1630–1714* (London: Peter Owens Publishers, 2010), 187–189.
6. Claudia Gold, *The King's Mistress: The True and Scandalous Story of the Woman Who Stole the Heart of George I*, (London: Quercus, 2012), 201. After the rift between George I and his son George August (later George II) in 1717, George August's children were left in the care of the king.
7. Juliane Moser and Tomke Stiasy, *Eutin Castle* (Berlin: Deutscher Kunstverlag, 2010), 29.
8. David McIntosh, *The Grand Dukes of Oldenburg* (Falköping: Rosvall Royal Books, 2007), 6.
9. Moser and Stiasy, *Eutin Castle*, 64.
10. McIntosh, *The Grand Dukes of Oldenburg*, 6.
11. Moser and Stiasy, *Eutin Castle*, 29.
12. Peter Coats, *The Great Gardens of Britain*. (London: Treasure Press, 1985.), 99.
13. McIntosh, *The Grand Dukes of Oldenburg*, 7.
14. Geoffrey Chamberlain, 'British Maternal Mortality in the 19th and early 20th Centuries', *Journal of the Royal Society of Medicine* (2006): Figure 1.
15. Leonard Bower and Gordon Bolitho, *Otho I: King of Greece, A Biography*, (London: Selwyn and Blount Ltd. Reprinted by *Royalty Digest* 2001), 90. Otto in a letter to his father of 15 August 1836.
16. Bower and Bolitho, *Otho I*, 91.
17. Jan Murken, 'Griechenland aus erster Hand: Konigin Amalie berichtet ihrem Vater'. Schriftenreihe des Otto Konig museums der Gemeinde Ottobrun, Nr14 (2013): 10.

18. Bower and Bolitho, *Otho I*, 174. 1848 report from Sir Stratford Canning to the British Foreign Secretary, Lord Palmerston.
19. Bower and Bolitho, *Otho I*, 224. In 1852 the British government sent a special mission to Greece to report on the situation and this quote is part of the report back.
20. Bower and Bolitho, *Otho I*, 101.
21. Murken, 'Griechenland aus erster Hand', 10.
22. Bower and Bolitho, *Otho I*, 132
23. Murken, 'Griechenland aus erster Hand', 11.
24. Wikipedia, 'Otto of Greece'.
25. Mary S. Lovell, *A Scandalous Life: The Biography of Jane Digby el Mezrab* (London: Richard Cohen Books, 1995), 101 and plate 20, opposite 176.
26. Bower and Bolitho, *Otho I*, 143. Lovell, *A Scandalous Life*, 131.
27. Lovell, *A Scandalous Life*, 141–143.
28. Bower and Bolitho, *Otho I*, 243.
29. Ibid, *Otho I*, 243.
30. Maren Siems, *The Princely Gallery in Jever Castle* (Schlossmuseum Jever, 2005), 10.
31. Robert K. Massie, *Catherine the Great: Portrait of a Woman* (London: Head of Zeus Ltd, 2013), 5.
32. Virginia Rounding, *Catherine the Great: Love, Sex and Power* (London: Hutchinson, 2006), 14.
33. Massie, *Catherine the Great*, 66.
34. Mark Cruse and Hilde Hoogenboom, *The Memoirs of Catherine the Great: A new translation by Mark Cruse and Hilde Hoogenboom* (New York: Modern Library, 2006), 26.
35. Cruse and Hoogenboom, *The Memoirs of Catherine the Great*, xii.
36. Massie, *Catherine the Great*, 252–3.
37. Cruse and Hoogenboom, *The Memoirs of Catherine the Great*, 31–2.

Chapter 3
38. Juliane Moser and Tomke Stiasy, *Eutin Castle* (Berlin: Dentscher Kunstverlag), 29.
39. Moser and Stiasy, *Eutin Castle*, 29. See also chapter 6 of this book (*Schloss II*) for Weimar as a cultural centre in the eighteenth and nineteenth centuries.
40. Moser and Stiasy, *Eutin Castle*, 8.
41. Moser and Stiasy, *Eutin Castle*, 2.
42. Virginia Rounding, *Catherine the Great: Love, Sex and Power* (London: Hutchinson, 2006), 63.

43. Robert K. Massie, *Catherine the Great: Portrait of a Woman* (London: Head of Zeus Ltd, 2013), 43.
44. Rounding, *Catherine the Great*, 303.
45. Massie, *Catherine the Great*, 471.
46. Sir Frederick Ponsonby, ed., *Letters of the Empress Frederick* (London: Macmillan and Co, 1928), 266.
47. David Duff, *Hessian Tapestry* (London: Frederick Muller, 1967), 222.
48. Duff, *Hessian Tapestry*, 213.
49. Duff, *Hessian Tapestry*, 289.
50. Robert K. Massie. *Nicholas & Alexandra: The Tragic Compelling Story of the Last Tsar and his Family* (London: Phoenix, reissued 2000), 346–348.
51. *The Times*, 'Prince Henry of Prussia: Obituary 22 April, 1929', Reprinted in *Royalty Digest: A Journal of Record* (1997): 360.
52. Anna Lerche and Marcus Mandal. *A Royal Family: The Story of Christian IX and his European Descendants* (Copenhagen: Egmont Lademann A/S/ Aschehoug, 2003), 54–55.
53. Lerche and Mandal, *A Royal Family*, 60 and 64.
54. Lerche and Mandal, *A Royal Family*, 62–63.
55. Lerche and Mandal, *A Royal Family*, 70.
56. Wolfgang J. Muller. *Glücksburg Castle* (Glücksburg: Siftung Schloss Glücksburg), 15.
57. Queen Victoria. *Queen Victoria in her Letters and Journals: A Selection by Christopher Hibbert* (New York: Viking, 1985), 181. Letter to the crown princess of Prussia dated 13 February 1864.
58. Zeichnung von Lene Brunsgård nach einem Entwurf von Hans Helmer Kristensen. Stammbaum Der Drei Herzogsdynastien. Museum Sønderjylland.
59. Discussion with Dr Ulf von Hielmcrone, chairman of the Society of Friends of Schloss vor Husum and president of the Nissen Foundation.
60. Discussion with Dr Ulf von Hielmcrone.
61. *Your Personal Guide to the Castle in Husum: Historical Background and Tour.* Schloss Husum.

Chapter 4
62. Gerlinde Kienitz, *Guidebook to Neustrelitz* (published by Stadt Neustrelitz), 2.
63. Olwen Hedley, *Queen Charlotte* (London: John Murray, 1975), 7.
64. Hedley, Queen Charlotte. 9.
65. John Watkins, *Memoirs of Sophia-Charlotte, Queen of Great Britain.* (London: Henry Colburn, 1819.), 81--82.

66. Hedley, *Queen Charlotte*. 44.
67. Watkins, *Memoirs of Sophia-Charlotte*. 104.
68. Stuart Jeffries, 'Was This Britain's First Black Queen?' *The Guardian* (12 March 2009).
69. Watkins, *Memoirs of Sophia-Charlotte*. 66–67.
70. Friederike Drinkuth, *Queen Charlotte: A Princess from Mecklenburg-Strelitz Ascends the Throne of England* (Schwerin: Thomas Helms Verlag, 2011), 36.
71. *Castles, Parks and Manor Houses: Royal Seats and Estate Villages in Mecklenburg-Vorpommern* (Rostock: Tourismusverband Mecklenburg-Vorpommern e.v., 2010), 17
72. *Castles, Parks and Manor Houses*, 22.
73. Marlies Schnaibel, *Luise: Queen of Prussia* (Karwe: Edition Rieger, 2005), 21.
74. Friederike Drinkuth, *English Landscape Garden Hohenzieritz* (Schwerin: Thomas Helms Verlag, 2009), 30.
75. Constance Wright, *Louise, Queen of Prussia: A Biography* (London: Frederick Muller, 1970), 229.
76. Schaibel, *Luise: Queen of Prussia*. 23.
77. Wright, *Louise, Queen of Prussia*, 234.
78. Drinkuth, *English Landscape Garden Hohenzieritz*, *inside cover and 1*.
79. Drinkuth, *English Landscape Garden Hohenzieritz*, 30.
80. Watkins, *Memoirs of Sophia-Charlotte*, 43–46. He takes this description from Thomas Nugent, who (Kienitz, *Guidebook to Neustrelitz*, 9) published a travel journal in 1766 called *Travels in Germany and Mainly in Mecklenburg*.
81. James Pope-Hennessy, *Queen Mary* (London: Phoenix Press, 2000), 98.
82. Cecil Woodham-Smith, *Queen Victoria: Her Life and Times, 1819–1861* (London: Hamish Hamilton, 1972), 233–234.
83. Bearn Bilker, 'Princess Elisabeth-Caroline zu Solms-Braunfels, 1916–2013', *Royalty Digest Quarterly* 3, 2013. 60. The princess was the daughter of Marie of Mecklenburg-Strelitz by her second marriage.
84. Ricardo Mateos Sainz de Medrano, 'L'Affaire Jametel', *Royalty Digest: A Journal of Record*, June 1999. 362.
85. Bilker, 'Princess Elisabeth-Caroline zu Solms-Braunfels', 61.
86. Pope-Hennessy, *Queen Mary*, 101.
87. Pope-Hennessy, *Queen Mary*, 100.
88. Pope-Hennessy, *Queen Mary*. 91–93.
89. Thomas Gehrlein, *Das Haus Mecklenburg* (Werl: Borde Verlag, 2012), 20.
90. *Castles, Parks and Manor Houses*, 46.

Chapter 5

91. Claudia Sommer and Detlef Fuchs, *Rheinsberg Palace* (Berlin: Stiftung Preussische Schlösser und Gärten Berlin-Brandenburg, Deutscher Kunstverlag, 2009), 4.
92. Clark, *Iron Kingdom*, 104; Note 68, cited in Reinhold Koser, *Friedrich der Grosse als Kronprinz.* (Stuttgart: 1886), 26.
93. David Fraser. *Frederick the Great: King of Prussia* (London: Allen Lane, The Penguin Press, 2000), 21.
94. Wilhelmina, Margravine of Bayreuth. *The Misfortunate Margravine: Early memoirs of Wilhelmina, Margravine of Bayreuth, Sister of Frederick the Great; with a Foreword by Pamela Hansford Johnson* (London: Macmillan and Co Ltd, 1970), 212.
95. Wilhelmina, *The Misfortunate Margravine*, 205.
96. Wilhelmina, *The Misfortunate Margravine*, 217–218.
97. Chester V. Easum, *Prince Henry of Prussia: Brother of Frederick the Great* (Wisconsin: The University of Wisconsin Press, 1942), 18.
98. Rheinsberg Palace audio guide.
99. Rheinsberg Palace audio guide.
100. Christopher Clark, *Iron Kingdom: The Rise and Downfall of Prussia 1600–1947* (London: Penguin Books, 2007), xxvi–xxix. Source Otto Büsch and Wolfgang Neugebauer (eds), *Moderne Preussische Geschichte 1648–1947: Eine Anthologie.* Berlin: Walter de Gruyter, 1981.
101. Rheinsberg Palace audio guide.
102. Easum, *Prince Henry of Prussia*, 51.

Chapter 6

103. Augusta, Duchess of Saxe-Coburg-Saalfeld, *In Napoleonic Days: Extracts from the Private Diary of Augusta, Duchess of Saxe-Coburg-Saalfeld, Queen Victoria's Maternal Grandmother, 1806–1821: Selected and Translated by H.R.H. the Princess Beatrice.* (London: John Murray, 1941), 1.
104. Augusta, *In Napoleonic Days*, 5–6.
105. Friedrich Wilhelm III was the grandson of Prince August Wilhelm who was disgraced by his elder brother Frederick the Great. Luis Ferdinand was the son of their youngest brother, Ferdinand. See chart 10.
106. Constance Wright, *Louise, Queen of Prussia: A Biography* (London: Frederick Muller, 1970), 120–121.
107. Augusta, *In Napoleonic Days*, 8.
108. Hanns Cibulka diary, *Späte Jahre* (late years), 2004. Quoted in Kamen Pawlow, *Gotha, A City Worth Visiting: Travel Guide Including Useful Information about Art, Nature and Sport* (Kamen Pawlow, self-published, 2008), 12.

109. Schloss Friedenstein audio guide.
110. Schloss Friedenstein audio guide.
111. Dulcie Ashdown, *Victoria and the Coburgs* (London: Robert Hale, 1981), 43.
112. *Memoirs of a Young Greek: Madame Pauline Adelaide Alexandre Panan against HRH the Reigning Prince of Saxe Coburg*. Mentioned in Richard Sotnick, *The Coburg Conspiracy: Victoria and Albert—Royal Plots and Manoeuvres* (Great Britain: Ephesus Publishing, 2010), 124.
113. Sotnick, *The Coburg Conspiracy*, 121–122.
114. Augusta, *In Napoleonic Days*, 180.
115. Sotnick, *The Coburg Conspiracy*, 148.
116. *DK Eyewitness Travel Guide, Germany* (London: DK, 2007), 190.
117. Queen Victoria's Journal, 5 Sept 1862. www.queenvictoriasjournal.org.
118. Christopher Hibbert, *Queen Victoria in Her Letters and Journals: A Selection by Christopher Hibbert* (New York: Viking, 1985), 157. Letter of 24 December 1861 from Queen Victoria to her uncle Leopold (her mother's brother), who was king of the Belgians.
119. Ibid, 163. Letter of 16 April 1862 from Queen Victoria to her eldest daughter, the crown princess of Prussia.
120. Ibid, 165. Letter of 25 June 1862 from Queen Victoria to the crown princess of Prussia.
121. Ibid, 162. Letter of 24 January 1862 from Queen Victoria to the crown princess of Prussia.
122. Clemens Beeck, *Weimar Highlights: The Practical Guide for Discovering the City* (Berlin: Jaron Verlag, 2012), 22.
123. Nicholas Boyle, *Goethe: The Poet and The Age, Volume I: The Poetry of Desire (1749–1790)* (Oxford: Clarendon Press, 1991), 233.
124. Rita Seifert, *Weimar: European Cultural Centre, Cradle of German Classicism*, 3rd edition (Lübeck: Schöning Verlag), 5.
125. Dorothee Ahrendt, *Belvedere Palace Park* (Weimar: Klassik Stiftung Weimar, 2009), inside the back cover.
126. William Mead Lalor, *The Daughters of Tsar Paul I, The Grand Duchesses: Daughters and Granddaughters of Russia's Tsars*, ed. Arturo E. Beéche (Oakland: Eurohistory.Com, 2004), 3.
127. Boyle, *Goethe Volume I*, vii.
128. Display board at Residenzschloss, Weimar.
129. Seifert, *Weimar*, 2–3.
130. Constance Wright, *Louise, Queen of Prussia: A Biography* (London: Frederick Muller, 1970), 119.
131. www.almanachdegotha.org. Principality of Schwarzburg-Rudolstadt.
132. Horst Fleischer and others. *Die Fürsten von Schwarzburg-*

Rudolstadt: 1710–1918. (Thüringer Landesmuseum Heidecksburg Rudolstadt, 2001.) Das Fürstenhaus von Schwarzburg-Rudolstadt (pullout genealogical chart).

133. The five children in the painting are Ludwig Friedrich b. 1767, Henriette b. 1770, Karl Günther b. 1771, Karoline b. 1774, and Louise b. 1775.
134. House Laws of Schwarzburg. www.heraldica.org
135. House Laws of Schwarzburg. www.heraldica.org
136. Charlotte Zeepvat, 'Schwarzburg-Rudolstadt: A Family Album', *Royalty Digest Quarterly* 2 (2014): 24.
137. *Schwarzburg Castle* (leaflet in English). Stiftung Thüringer Schlösser und Gärten and Landkreis Saalfeld-Rudolstadt.
138. *Schatzkammer Thüringen: The Heritage of Princely Culture* (leaflet in English). Stiftung Thüringer Schlösser und Gärten.
139. Gerlinde Gräfin von Westphalen, *Anna Luise von Schwarzburg: Die Letzte Fürstin.* (Jena: Jenzig-Verlag Gabriele Köhler, 2011.)
140. Von Westphalen, *Anna Luise von Schwarzburg*, 8.
141. Von Westphalen, *Anna Luise von Schwarzburg*, 11.

Chapter 7
142. Lord Edmond Fitzmaurice, *Charles William Ferdinand, Duke of Brunswick: An Historical Study, 1735–1806* (London: Longmans Green and Co, 1901), 2.
143. Augusta, Duchess of Saxe-Coburg-Saalfeld, *In Napoleonic Days: Extracts from the Private Diary of Augusta, Duchess of Saxe-Coburg-Saalfeld, Queen Victoria's Maternal Grandmother, 1806–1821: Selected and Translated by H.R.H. the Princess Beatrice* (London: John Murray, 1941), 10.
144. Flora Fraser, *The Unruly Queen: The Life of Queen Caroline.* (London: Macmillan, 1996.), 58.
145. Fitzmaurice, *Charles William Ferdinand, Duke of Brunswick*, 17.
146. Virginia Rounding, *Catherine the Great: Love, Sex and Power* (London: Hutchinson, 2006), 419–421.
147. Fraser, *The Unruly Queen*, 174 (quoted from the Royal Archives).
148. Fitzmaurice, *Charles William Ferdinand, Duke of Brunswick*, 16 (footnote).
149. Fraser, *The Unruly Queen*, 443. This popular ditty apparently arose out of her defence counsel's closing speech.
150. Robert K. Massie, *Catherine the Great: Portrait of a Woman* (London: Head of Zeus Ltd, 2013), 10.
151. J. N. Duggan, *Sophia of Hanover: From Winter Princess to Heiress of Great Britain, 1630–1714* (London: Peter Owen Publishers, 2010), 139.
152. Maria Kroll, *Sophie: Electress of Hanover: A Personal Portrait*

(London: Victor Gollancz Ltd, 1973), 178.

153. Kroll, *Sophie*, 238.

154. Hans-Henning Grote, *Wolfenbüttel Palace: Residence of the Dukes of Brunswick and Lüneburg* (Braunschweig: Appelhans, 2008), 24.

155. Kroll, *Sophie*, 237.

156. Heinrich Zschokke, *The Princess of Brunswick-Wolfenbüttel and Other Tales: Collection of German Authors, Vol 8* (Leipzig: Bernhard Tauchnitz, 1867).

157. Zschokke, *The Princess of Brunswick-Wolfenbüttel*, 25.

158. Peter Munz, *Frederick Barbarossa: A Study in Medieval Politics* (London: Eyre and Spottiswoode, 1969), 3.

159. Joachim Zeune, *Castles and Palaces: Germany* (Regensburg: Schmidt Verlag, 2004), 42.

160. *The Goslar Kaiserpfalz: The Vaults, an Introduction to Goslar Imperial History* (English handout).

161. *The Goslar Kaiserpfalz*.

162. *The Goslar Kaiserpfalz*.

163. Claudia Gold, *The King's Mistress: The True and Scandalous Story of the Woman Who Stole the Heart of George I* (London: Quercus, 2012), 259–264.

164. Peter Steckhan, *700 Years Wolfsburg Castle* (leaflet in English). Stadtmuseum Schloss Wolfsburg.

165. David Fraser, *Fredrick the Great: King of Prussia* (London: Allen Lane, The Penguin Press, 2000), 29.

166. Hans Adolf Schultz, *Burgen, Schlösser und Herrensitze im Raum Gifhorn-Wolfsburg*, Schriftenreihe zur Heimatkunde der Sparkasse Gifhorn-Wolfsburg, Band I. 63.

Chapter 8

167. *Time To Travel: Travel in Time to Germany's Finest Stately Homes, Gardens, Castles, Abbeys and Roman Remains* (Regensburg: Schnell and Steiner, 2010). *Schencks Castles and Gardens: Historic Houses and Heritage Sights* (Hamburg: Schenck Verlag, 2012).

Appendix D

168. German Confederation. Wikipedia, the free encyclopaedia. Note (4), Heeren, Arnold Hermann Ludwig (1873), Talboys, David Alphonso, ed.; *A Manual of the History of the Political System of Europe and its Colonies* (London: H.G. Bohn), 480–481.

169. Viktoria Luise, Duchess of Brunswick and Lüneburg, *The Kaiser's Daughter: Memoirs of HRH Viktoria Luise, Duchess of Brunswick and Lüneburg, Princess of Prussia* (London: W H Allen and Co, 1977).

THE SCHLOSS SERIES OF BOOKS

Schloss is the German word for castle or palace, and you are never far from one of these in Germany. For most of its history Germany was not a single country but a patchwork of royal states, held together under the banner of the Holy Roman Empire. The dukes and princes who ruled these states were passionate builders. Their beautiful castles and palaces, and their compelling personal stories, provide the material for the *Schloss* series of books.

This book can be seen as an inspiration ... to get out there and find the lesser known palaces and learn more about their history. Royalty Digest Quarterly Journal.

Each of the *Schloss* books includes twenty-five beautiful castles and palaces in Germany and looks at these from two perspectives. The first is the author's experience as an overseas visitor to each schloss; the second, colourful stories of the historical royal families connected with them. Royalty have always been the celebrities of their day, and these stories from history can rival anything in modern-day television soap operas.

The second volume is as good as the first, maybe even better – a must... Amazon review.

THE SCHLOSS SERIES OF BOOKS

The stories in the *Schloss* books include the mistress of the king who tried to blackmail him and was imprisoned for forty-nine years; the princess from a tiny German state who used her body and her brains to become the ruler of the vast Russian empire; the prince who defied his family to marry a pharmacist's daughter and then bought her the rank of royal princess; and the duke whose personal story is so colourful he has been called the Bavarian Henry VIII!

Susan Symons has done another fantastic job, proving the point that history can also be fun...
The European Royal History Journal.

The German princes abdicated in 1918, at the end of World War I, and Germany became a republic. As they lost their royal families, many castles and palaces went into decline and became prisons, workhouses, and other institutions. Some were damaged or destroyed in World War II; others lay behind the Iron Curtain for fifty years. The books chart these difficult years and their resurgence and use today as public buildings, museums, and hotels.

The latest addition visits Bavaria – and what a treat it is. Fascinating reading!
The European Royal History Journal

THE SCHLOSS SERIES OF BOOKS

The castles and palaces in the books range in time from fortified castles of the middle-ages; to grand palaces built in imitation of Louis XIV's Versailles; to stately homes from the turn of the early twentieth century. Many are not well known outside Germany and some rarely see an English-speaking visitor. The *Schloss* books might encourage you to go and see these wonderful places for yourself.

The books are sympathetic to our fascinating German royal history and make linkages and connections in a clear and interesting way.
European Castles Institute, Schloss Philippsburg, Germany.

The *Schloss* books are intended to be light-hearted and easy to read. Illustrated throughout and supplemented with charts and family trees, they should appeal to anyone who likes history or sightseeing or is interested in people's personal stories. With dozens of royal families in Germany before the monarchy fell, there are still many more castles and palaces to go, and Susan is already at work on the next book.

This is a well-written, entertaining display of the castles ... I am definitely off to Thuringia, Symons' book in hand.
Royalty Digest Quarterly Journal

SCHLOSS WURZACH
A JERSEY CHILD INTERNED BY HITLER
– GLORIA'S STORY

In the early hours of 16 September 1942 there was a knock on the door of ten-year-old Gloria Webber's home in Jersey. Gloria, her parents and four younger children were all on a list of Jersey civilians to be

deported to Germany on the direct orders of Hitler. Gloria and her siblings, with hundreds of other Jersey children, spent the next years of their childhood interned in an old castle in the south of Germany, called Schloss Wurzach.

Schloss Wurzach was a grand baroque palace built in the eighteenth century by one of Germany's noble families. But by World War II it had fallen on hard times and was used as a prison camp. The schloss was cold, damp, in poor condition, and very dirty. The internees were horrified by what they found. Twelve of the islanders died in Wurzach during their detention and are buried in the town; others suffered fractured lives.

This short book recalls Gloria's childhood experience and is illustrated with vivid pictures of camp life painted by her father during their confinement. It also describes how she and other internees returned to Germany in later life to celebrate their liberation with the people of Wurzach, showing there can be reconciliation and friendship between former enemies.

THE COLOURFUL PERSONAL LIFE OF QUEEN VICTORIA

Queen Victoria is the British monarch in history who's name everyone knows. These three books focus on the Queen as a woman – her personal life, events that formed her resolute character, and relationships that were important to her. They use some of her own words from her journal, to help tell the story; and are illustrated with portraits and memorabilia from the author's own collection.

Victoria has a life story full of drama, intrigue and surprises. *Young Victoria* covers the bizarre events of her birth, with a scramble to produce the heir to the throne; her lonely childhood under a tough regime; and how she came to the throne at 18.

Victoria & Albert is the story of her marriage to Albert and how she balanced the roles of monarch and Victorian wife and mother. *The Widowed Queen* covers the long years of her life alone after Albert's early death, when she became an icon of the age; the longest serving European sovereign; and matriarch of a huge clan.

Made in United States
North Haven, CT
13 May 2023

36530581R00137